C000061738

Russell K....

Series Introduction

The *Major Conservative and Libertarian Thinkers* series aims to show that there is a rigorous, scholarly tradition of social and political thought that may be broadly described as "conservative", "libertarian" or some combination of the two.

The series aims to show that conservatism is not simply a reaction against contemporary events, nor a privileging of intuitive thought over deductive reasoning; libertarianism is not simply an apology for unfettered capitalism or an attempt to justify a misguided atomistic concept of the individual. Rather, the thinkers in this series have developed coherent intellectual positions that are grounded in empirical reality and also founded upon serious philosophical reflection on the relationship between the individual and society, how the social institutions necessary for a free society are to be established and maintained, and the implications of the limits to human knowledge and certainty.

Each volume in the series presents a thinker's ideas in an accessible and cogent manner to provide an indispensable work for students with varying degrees of familiarity with the topic as well as more advanced scholars.

The following twenty volumes that make up the entire *Major Conservative and Libertarian Thinkers* series are written by international scholars and experts:

The Salamanca School by Andre Azevedo Alves (LSE, UK) and
    José Manuel Moreira (Universidade de Aveiro, Portugal)
Thomas Hobbes by R. E. R. Bunce (Cambridge, UK)
John Locke by Eric Mack (Tulane, UK)
David Hume by Christopher J. Berry (Glasgow, UK)
Adam Smith by James Otteson (Yeshiva, US)
Edmund Burke by Dennis O'Keeffe (Buckingham, UK)
Alexis de Tocqueville by Alan S Kahan (Paris, France)
Herbert Spencer by Alberto Mingardi (Istituto Bruno Leoni, Italy)

Ludwig von Mises by Richard Ebeling (Northwood, US)
Joseph A. Schumpeter by John Medearis (Riverside, California, US)
F. A. Hayek by Adam Tebble (UCL, UK)
Michael Oakeshott by Edmund Neill (Oxford, UK)
Karl Popper by Phil Parvin (Cambridge, UK)
Ayn Rand by Mimi Gladstein (Texas, US)
Milton Friedman by William Ruger (Texas State, US)
Russell Kirk by John Pafford (Northwood, US)
James M. Buchanan by John Meadowcroft (King's College London, UK)
The Modern Papacy by Samuel Gregg (Acton Institute, US)
Murray Rothbard by Gerard Casey (UCD, Ireland)
Robert Nozick by Ralf Bader (St Andrews, UK)

Of course, in any series of this nature, choices have to be made as to which thinkers to include and which to leave out. Two of the thinkers in the series – F. A. Hayek and James M. Buchanan – have written explicit statements rejecting the label "conservative". Similarly, other thinkers, such as David Hume and Karl Popper, may be more accurately described as classical liberals than either conservatives or libertarians. But these thinkers have been included because a full appreciation of this particular tradition of thought would be impossible without their inclusion; conservative and libertarian thought cannot be fully understood without some knowledge of the intellectual contributions of Hume, Hayek, Popper and Buchanan, among others. While no list of conservative and libertarian thinkers can be perfect, then, it is hoped that the volumes in this series come as close as possible to providing a comprehensive account of the key contributors to this particular tradition.

John Meadowcroft
King's College London

Russell Kirk

John M. Pafford

Major Conservative and Libertarian Thinkers

Series Editor: John Meadowcroft

B L O O M S B U R Y
NEW YORK · LONDON · NEW DELHI · SYDNEY

Bloomsbury Academic
An imprint of Bloomsbury Publishing Plc

1385 Broadway	50 Bedford Square
New York	London
NY 10018	WC1B 3DP
USA	UK

www.bloomsbury.com

Hardback edition first published in 2011 by the Continuum International
Publishing Group Inc.

This paperback edition published by Bloomsbury Academic 2013

© John M. Pafford, 2013

All rights reserved. No part of this publication may be reproduced or
transmitted in any form or by any means, electronic or mechanical, including
photocopying, recording, or any information storage or retrieval system,
without prior permission in writing from the publishers.

No responsibility for loss caused to any individual or organization acting on
or refraining from action as a result of the material in this publication can be
accepted by Bloomsbury Academic or the author.

Library of Congress Cataloging-in-Publication Data
A catalog record for this book is available from the Library of Congress.

ISBN: HB:	978-1-4411-9569-2
PB:	978-1-4411-6557-2
ePub:	978-1-6235-6219-9

Typeset by Newgen Imaging Systems Pvt Ltd, Chennai, India
Printed and bound in the United States of America

Contents

Series Editor's Preface

Russell Kirk was one of the principal intellectual architects of the American conservative movement in the second half of the twentieth century and beyond. In numerous works of philosophy and fiction published over five decades Kirk set out a vision of the United States in particular and Western civilization more generally as a social order founded upon an inherited tradition of values in which Christian theology played a crucial role. Kirk wrote of a moral order that transcended human judgment and intelligence; permanent moral truths did exist that if adhered to could create an inner harmony of the soul and an outer harmony of society. These truths were to be found within the customs, conventions, and continuities of societies that embodied the accumulated wisdom of many generations and reflected a divinely-inspired natural order.

Kirk's conservatism, then, can be located firmly in the Burkean tradition that warns of the dangers of destroying social institutions that may not satisfy the demands of rational analysis but nevertheless perform an important social function that may not always be easily identified or articulated. For example, although gradations of status and class may upset modern egalitarian sensibilities, Kirk warned that the destruction of such natural distinctions disturbs the natural order of things and may leave a vacuum to be filled by oligarchs and tyrants. Hence, for Kirk, reason was an important human quality, but it is a mistake to place so much faith in reason that we become blind to the presence of an over-arching and transcendent moral framework that orders human affairs.

In this excellent book, Professor John Pafford of Northwood University, a former student and friend of Russell Kirk, sets out Kirk's thought in the context of Kirk's life and times. He shows how an appreciation of Kirk's careful synthesis of theology and philosophy is crucial to an understanding of modern American conservatism and contemporary conservative thought more generally. The author also sets out the sometimes strained relationship between Kirk's conservatism and libertarian ideas. By so doing, this volume makes a crucial contribution to the *Major Conservative and Libertarian Thinkers* series. It is a book that will prove indispensable to those unfamiliar with Kirk's work as well as more advanced scholars.

John Meadowcroft
King's College London

List of Abbreviations

1

Introduction

Assuming that the person being evaluated is honest, what that individual has to say about himself or herself should be the beginning point for the study; the words then should be analyzed in the light of what is known concerning how that person lived. With people of integrity, there is consistency between profession and practice. Anyone who knew Russell Kirk knew such a man. Although those who write about themselves are trying to shape how future generations will view them, the Russell Kirk who is found in his memoirs as well as in his fiction and nonfiction writings does not differ from the man known to his family, friends, and colleagues. In my case, I not only read Kirk's works, but the privilege was mine to have had him as a mentor and as a friend.

I first encountered Kirk's writings in 1968. At that time, I was teaching history at Highland College, a now defunct Christian institution in Pasadena, California, and working part-time as a research analyst at the Christian Freedom Foundation in Los Angeles. Howard Kershner was the president and G. Edward Rowe the executive director—the man who hired me. One of my assignments was to read Kirk's *Enemies of the Permanent Things* and give Rowe a synopsis of it. This book made a deep impact on me. Here were clear and profound thoughts on our past and present; I experienced a sense of intellectual excitement, of understanding with greater lucidity what hitherto had been more dimly perceived.

My meeting Kirk did not happen until November 1976 after my family and I moved to Midland, Michigan where I began my still continuing association with Northwood University as a professor of history. We arrived in August of that year. It took me several weeks to settle in and attempt to contact the man who had become my intellectual hero. I supposed that someone of his prominence either had an unlisted telephone number or, if not, would be difficult to approach. On both counts I was wrong. After getting his number from information, I called his home, asked for him, and introduced myself. He thereupon invited my wife and me for Sunday afternoon tea, commencing almost two decades of inspiration, guidance, and friendship.

The one hour drive from Midland to Kirk's residence in Mecosta was enjoyable, especially going by the farmland, open fields, and scattered groves of trees in the rolling countryside between Mount Pleasant and Mecosta. The latter is a small town, now past its prime which was back in the 1880s when lumbering in Michigan was at its peak. Today the village stretches a couple of blocks along both sides of a wide part of Michigan route 20. Those who drive through the village heading west go up a slight rise, at the top of which on the left is the Kirk residence, Piety Hill, a large brick edifice with gargoyles, out of place in this community of smaller, mostly wood frame homes. Down the side street by the Kirk residence are several houses owned by a foundation supporting Kirk and his library which housed about 12,000 volumes.

Kirk himself turned out to be a genial gentleman of medium height and slightly rotund. In social settings he was rather shy although he could be coaxed into telling stories, he being a gifted raconteur. Generally, though, he did not control the flow of conversation, his wife Annette and frequently voluble guests handling that.

A couple of years later, Kirk informed me of his connection with International College in California, an institution with no central campus which brought together outstanding scholars and students, the students traveling to wherever the master tutor lived and spending as much time as necessary in residence to complete a prescribed course of study for a degree. Associated with International College, in addition to Kirk, were such luminaries as Eric von Kuehnelt-Leddihn, Anais Nin, Buckminster Fuller, Laurence Durrell, and Yehudi Menuhin.

For somewhat over 4 years, I studied under Kirk for my Ph.D. in history. Generally I stayed in my office at Northwood weekdays after completing my teaching assignments, reading and writing until dinner and devoted most Saturdays to further research and writing. One or two Saturdays each month I drove to Mecosta to report on my progress and to sit enthralled in the Kirk library while he continued to amaze me with the breadth and depth of his knowledge and wisdom. Between sessions we had lunch, sometimes with other people visiting Piety Hill. Among those making pilgrimages to Mecosta were the grandson of the last Austro-Hungarian emperor, and people who had fled Communism such as two young members of one of the Ethiopian noble families, a Polish professor, a government official from Croatia, and former members of the South Vietnamese armed forces. Also well-known individuals such as William F. Buckley and Malcolm Muggeridge journeyed there. Warm hospitality always was to be found at Piety Hill as were informative and stimulating seminars. Suffusing everything there was a palpable aura of Christian civilization.

2

The Life of Russell Kirk

Early Years[1]

Russell Amos Kirk was born on October 19, 1918, just over 3 weeks before the allied powers forced Germany to acknowledge defeat, bringing World War I to an end. The empires of Germany, Austria-Hungary, Russia, and Turkey were no more. In their places were chaos and/or newer, smaller, weaker countries with the exception of the Turkish Empire whose sway over most of the Middle East was replaced by British and, to a lesser extent, French dominance. The victorious European powers—the United Kingdom, France, and Italy—were battered physically and psychologically in the wake of 4 years of bloody conflict. But, the United States into which Kirk was born had emerged stronger economically, militarily, and in terms of overall power and prestige. It was filled with vibrant, confident people. Yet, this time of great technological advancement also was a time when many foundational beliefs of Western Civilization increasingly were being challenged. Dull times did not lie ahead.

Kirk's parents were of middling means, his father a railroad engineer with less than 6 years of schooling, his mother the daughter of a restaurateur, later bank manager. The family home was near the rail yards in Plymouth,

Michigan, a suburb of Detroit. Seven years later, a sister, Carolyn, joined the family. They lived in a bungalow-style house on a tree-shaded street, a solid middle-class community with, by and large, honest, hardworking family people.

Coming close to death from nephritis, a serious kidney inflammation, Kirk was a sickly child until age 7. At first read to by his mother and her father, Frank Pierce, he later became a voracious reader. Young Kirk and his maternal grandfather became close, taking long walks together and discussing serious matters. Frank Pierce, a bank manager in Plymouth, had attended college for only one term, but had educated himself quite extensively, being especially interested in history. His home had the works of Macaulay, Dickens, Victor Hugo, and Mark Twain. Kirk, encountering great books and being given copies of them at early ages, became enthralled by the world of ideas and imagination. He retained happy memories of his childhood, especially of generations of family members interacting.

He attended the public schools of Plymouth beginning in 1922, a time when public education was substantially different. Kirk commented on his experiences there, writing that:

> From kindergarten to graduation day, he[2] took it for granted that schools were orderly, safe, and reasonably pleasant places—an assumption that would be dispelled swiftly in most public schools seven decades later. (TSI, 25)

On a deeper level, even though the public schools did not seek to inculcate Christian verities, Kirk recalled:

Yet Christian morals were taken for granted. Nearly all the teachers belonged to one denomination or another—Presbyterian, Methodist, Lutheran, and Baptist chiefly; their assumptions about ultimate questions were derived from Christian doctrine; but dogmatic instruction was left entirely to the several Sunday schools of the churches. (TSI, 27)

A general Christian consensus still pervaded the culture in which Kirk grew up.

Kirk's parents were people of staunch integrity and morality, but did not attend church. His great-grandparents on his mother's side, the Johnsons of Mecosta, were Spiritualists, intrigued by the writings of Emanuel Swedenborg.[3] Séances were held in their home which occupied the site of the present Piety Hill. Kirk wrote of strange experiences while visiting his great-grandmother and her two unmarried daughters. He recounted the events of one night he was visiting them during the Christmas season when he was eight or nine in age. The house being crowded with relatives, he had settled in for the night on a sofa in the front parlor, when suddenly he saw two men outside the bay window in the snow looking in. One was tall and bearded, the other short. Too scared to investigate further, he hid under the covers and drifted into sleep. His resolve strengthened by the coming of day, he checked outside, but found no footprints in the snow. Years later, as part of a casual conversation with his aunt Fay (his mother's sister) she mentioned having two men seen by no one else with whom she played as a little girl outside that very parlor window. One, she said, was tall and bearded, the other short and clean-shaven. The first she called Dr. Cady, the other Patti.

To continue this rather singular tale, still later, Kirk's oldest daughter, Monica, then 2 years old, was observed waving to others present, and shouting, "Hi, Patti! Hi, Patti!" She said that he was a short man. In discussing these happenings, Kirk made only a cryptic reference to "thin places" in this world "where something may be glimpsed as through a veil." (TSI, 27) He did once comment in conversation with me that he believed it likely that encounters of this nature were with those who had left this world, but for some reason had not yet gone to their final place.

Overall, the young Kirk was by no means religious. He stated of himself: "Skeptical from early years, in his teens he would twit his elders by professing militant atheism; actually he was too skeptical to accept atheism's dogmata." (TSI, 14) It would be years before reason would be subordinated to revelation. During his college years, he read such classical thinkers as Marcus Aurelius, Epictetus, and Seneca as part of his self-education. While serving in Utah during World War II, he read them again. As a student, Kirk was erratic, drawn to history and English literature, less to math, science, and foreign languages. He remembered graduating about ninth in a class of about 100. Little interested in team sports, he did, though, develop in his youth a love of the strenuous life, exemplified by his running a mile to school in the morning, coming home for lunch at the same pace, running back to school afterwards, and vigorous scuffling and play after school (TSI, 14). Bookish he may have been, but a keen sense of adventure was a powerful force in his life, manifested by his wandering on foot up to 40 miles per day through Utah, the European continent, and the British Isles and in characters in his novels such as the soldier, scholar, statesman Manfred Arcane.

While in high school, his skill in writing began to attract notice. In 1932, he won the *Detroit Times* gold medal for his essay on the bicentenary of Washington's birth. Four years later, *Scholastic* magazine awarded him first prize in their national essay contest.

Kirk graduated from high school in 1936, a time when the Great Depression still firmly gripped the country. Few promising employment prospects lay ahead for him. Working for the railroad, as did his father, did not attract him. His interest in and facility in writing opened the possibility of a newspaper job, but that did not materialize. His high school principal suggested that he take the examination for a scholarship to Michigan State College of Agriculture and Applied Science (later Michigan State University). He won and matriculated there. His family unable to help him financially, his savings from part-time jobs only $200, and his scholarship covering only tuition, Kirk faced the literal poor student existence. He subsisted on one main meal per day, filling in with peanut butter and crackers.

The overall level of student intellectual interest he found low, leavened though by some sharp young members of the faculty and a few students with enthusiasm for learning. Above all, he read voraciously in a wide variety of areas, including outside his courses. In order to have this time, he rejected opportunities to live better by taking part-time jobs during the academic year. Kirk believed that student poverty was a price worth paying in return for the time to read and to think. He did win competitions for essays, short stories, and speaking. The small cash prizes helped with his living expenses and the process enhanced his intellectual growth.

Beginning in 1937, Kirk worked summers as a guide at Greenfield Village in Dearborn. The vision of Henry Ford, it was a collection of historic buildings and replicas, reproducing an earlier era. Kirk's uncle, Glenn "Potter" Jewell, had been an assistant to Ford and arranged this opportunity for his nephew. Intrigued by Greenfield Village, Kirk continued his summer employment there through the summer of 1941. Graduating from Michigan State in 1940, a history major, Kirk applied to Pennsylvania State University and to Duke University in order to study for his M.A. Both accepted him, but Duke offered him an assistantship which provided free tuition and a stipend. He was impressed with Duke academically and by the impressive buildings on the campus. Here he developed a love for the traditionalism and the civility of the South. Of his professors, he especially appreciated Charles Sydnor in Southern history and Jay Hubbell in Southern literature. His master's thesis, later published as his first book, *Randolph of Roanoke*, dealt with this significant figure from the early years of the United States.

In 1941, master's degree in hand, he returned to Greenfield Village. Germany now dominated Europe and Japanese aggression in Asia was moving at a more rapid pace. It did not appear that the United States much longer would be on the sidelines. For Kirk, Ph.D. studies would have to wait. After Pearl Harbor, Greenfield Village was closed down until after the war ended and Kirk was transferred to the River Rouge Plant, assigned to the payroll department at the new aircraft engine building. He attempted to become a pilot in the Army Air Corps, but his eyes were not up to their standard. In the summer of 1942, the army drafted him and a new chapter opened.

After going to the induction center in Detroit, Kirk was assigned to the now defunct Camp Custer in southern Michigan. Shortly thereafter he and 100 other new soldiers were assigned to the Chemical Warfare Service and sent to Dugway Proving Ground in the Great Salt Lake Desert of Utah about 90 miles from Salt Lake City. Although poison gas was not used during World War II, the United States prepared in case the eventuality arose. After all, gas had been employed extensively during World War I and the Italians had gassed the Ethiopians during the 1935–1936 conflict. Also worked on at Dugway were the gel bomb and bacteriological warfare capabilities. Kirk did suffer minor problems from mustard gas and phosgene mishaps, but overall found his 3 years in the desert healthful. He was assigned to office duty, but had leisure time for reading and exploring the peaks and valleys of the surrounding countryside. The solitude of the post did not weigh on him as it did on some others.

While serving there, he renewed his reading from his college years of Marcus Aurelius, Epictetus, and Seneca, being drawn especially to the Stoicism[4] of Marcus Aurelius and Zeno. It also was at this time that Kirk read Albert Jay Nock's *Memoirs of a Superfluous Man*. Nock was a former Episcopal priest who had moved away from Christian foundational beliefs to become a libertarian curmudgeon. They discussed Marcus Aurelius in letters, but this was not for long a stopping point in Kirk's spiritual odyssey.

When Kirk's mother died in 1942, he wrote of himself that then "Kirk knew next to nothing about any religion. Perhaps the vanishing of Marjorie Pierce Kirk began to wake him to some awareness of the eternal and the sacred." (TSI, 66) Yet the journey would be long before basic Christianity would bloom within him. He would progress slowly from young freethinker to belief in a generalized theism, to support for civilizational Christianity (an appreciation of Christianity as the foundation of Western Civilization), to ultimately a genuinely held personal faith.

Meanwhile, World War II continued and Kirk remained in uniform, part of a little known military operation in a well off-the-beaten path part of the world. His sense of adventure was satisfied to some extent by his wandering, sometimes alone, sometimes with companions, through the rugged high desert and mountain terrain of Utah. He reveled in physical challenges and the development of physical toughness. At the same time, he was growing in mind and spirit.

In late 1944 into early 1945, Kirk was part of a detachment sent from Dugway to Florida, to a swampy area north of Tampa near Bushnell to test the effect of mustard gas on soldiers. Not to anyone's surprise, it was determined that unprotected personnel walking through brush sprayed with mustard gas can suffer serious burns. The unit then was returned to Utah where Kirk resumed his dealing with classified documents. In 1946, he was discharged, a staff sergeant.

Life in Academe

Returning to his roots in Plymouth and Mecosta, Kirk was rather at loose ends, pondering the direction he should take. The world of commerce held little appeal. At this time, in spite of his love of books and the camaraderie with those of like mind, the academic life did not loom large in his thinking. Law exerted a powerful attraction, but law school was expensive, Kirk's funds limited, and scholarships few. Then, in an East Lansing restaurant, one of his former Michigan State history professors encountered him, inquired of his plans, and finding him unengaged, set in motion the process which resulted in Kirk's joining the college faculty to teach the history of civilization in the newly opened Basic College. He taught there one semester each year until 1953. Its intent, as Kirk explained it, was to provide remedial education, teaching those who in previous generations would not have been pursuing higher education. Here expectations were low in terms of reading and writing. With the new G. I. Bill and millions of returning veterans, colleges were expanding rapidly. Many benefited from this, but Kirk found himself teaching large sections with up to 100 students, a large percentage of whom wanted degrees, but were not much interested in serious learning. There were some colleagues Kirk respected and some good students, but, overall, educational standards at Michigan State did not impress him (TSI, 76–79).

This experience sparked serious inquiry into education by Kirk which culminated over the years in a number of articles, essays, and books. It also stimulated a probing by him of alternative ways to earn a living while simultaneously doing something to enhance intellectual standards. He did recognize the necessity of supporting himself, although as a bachelor and one more oriented to ideas and adventure, it did not dominate his thinking. He and a friend opened a used book store in East Lansing, intending both to supplement his Michigan State income and encourage the reading of good books while meeting and conversing with interesting people. They operated the Red Cedar Bookshop for 2 years. Although he enjoyed much from the experience, Kirk found that it absorbed a lot of his time and was not profitable. Also, the wish to travel and to pursue a doctoral program moved back to the fore as he thought ahead to the next chapter of his life. US graduate schools struck him as "pedantic, bureaucratic, and given to excessive supervision." (TSI, 82) Discovering a book about St. Andrews University in Scotland opened to him prospects of travel, adventure, and study at one of the great universities of the Western World, free from the stifling rigidity of so many American programs. So, the combination of these factors propelled him out of the deadening routine of Michigan State across the Atlantic to St. Andrews where he could study more freely and live cheaper than at an American institution. Here, at the oldest university in Scotland and the third oldest in Britain, he thrived in an atmosphere of academic freedom, unbound by mandated courses and examinations; the doctoral dissertation would determine all. His rewarding, pleasurable years here led to his history of St. Andrews, the city as well as the university, which was published in 1954.

From 1948 through 1952, Kirk divided each year one semester at Michigan State earning income, the rest of the year in the Old World, studying, growing, and experiencing Europe, whenever possible walking which he considered the best way to get to know a country. He especially enjoyed tramping through Britain, most especially Scotland. The traditionalism, deep civilizational roots, and humane pace were most congenial to him. This exemplified his belief in the unity of Western Civilization, particularly the common foundational principles of both Britain and the United States. He was a patriotic American, aware of national differences, but viewed what drew together the West as more important than what divided it.

His work at St. Andrews was directed by Professor John Williams Williams. Both he and the university accepted Kirk's dissertation, later to be published as *The Conservative Mind*,[5] his second published work, *Randolph of Roanoke: A Study in Conservative Thought* which came out in 1951, being the first. Kirk now in 1952 was awarded his D.Litt., doctor of letters, the only American to have received this, the highest degree awarded by this venerable institution.

After another semester at Michigan State, Kirk had had enough of the increasing focus there on numerical growth and the consequent lowering of academic standards. From now on, his reputation established by *The Conservative Mind*, he supported himself and his later family as a writer, a speaker, and as an occasional visiting professor.

Scholar and Squire

After severing ties with Michigan State, Kirk moved north to Mecosta where stood Piety Hill, the large white clapboard house built by his great-grandfather Amos Johnson. Now the house and 40 acres were owned by Glenn Jewell who had married Fay Pierce, sister of Kirk's mother; they lived in a cabin next door to Piety Hill. Still living in the old house were Eva Pierce, Kirk's widowed grandmother, and Norma and Frances Johnson, his unmarried great-aunts, daughters of Amos and Estella Johnson. Shortly after arriving, Kirk bought the house and accompanying property for $6,000. On the upper floor, he fixed himself a library/study, a bedroom, and a bath. His aged relatives continued to live in the house, receiving from him a monthly stipend.

Down the side street beside the house was a large brick building which previously had been a small factory making oak stools for children and cigarette-rollers. This, Kirk purchased and converted into his library, the room at Piety Hill now proving to be too small. From across the country and, indeed, from around the world, came people to study and attend conferences there. Today, years after the death of Russell Kirk, the library continues as a vibrant center for all that he believed and taught.

Kirk's father and stepmother lived in Baldwin, north and west of Mecosta, in a home he purchased for them. The older Kirk still worked as a railroad engineer. Later, after retirement, they moved to Mecosta and lived next door to Piety Hill. Under the reserved, shy exterior, the younger Kirk was a deeply sentimental man, not the natural loner he sometimes appeared to be and sometimes was.

During the next decade, Kirk continued writing books, articles, and columns, and serving as a visiting professor at various institutions such as Vanderbilt University, Pepperdine University, the University of Colorado, Central Michigan University, and Hillsdale College. He also traveled extensively through the British Isles, on the continent of Europe, and in North Africa. He made a point of walking through these lands, considering that the best way to know countries, especially the people in them. In addition, Kirk was active in his community, spending several years as a justice of the peace, a position which no longer exists in Michigan. In this, he was furthering a family tradition of service. For example, his great-grandfather, Amos Johnson, had been Mecosta village president and Mecosta County judge of probate. Grandfather Frank Pierce was a village commissioner and president of the school board in Plymouth and uncle Glenn Jewell was Morton township (Mecosta village was part of the township) supervisor and a member of the Mecosta County board of supervisors. These were not positions of power from which great decisions were made affecting the course of nations, but, without capable, honest people in these posts, no country would long survive; they are part of the essential foundation on which national greatness is built. Kirk, though, would rise above this solid bourgeois level. Beyond the family tradition, he, widely read and well-traveled with deep roots in Scotland and England, exemplified the noblesse oblige characteristic of the British gentry. He embodied the best qualities of this class—integrity, service to the community, a sense of the interconnectedness of past, present, and future. He never denied or even attempted to cover over his relatively modest origins, but he did enjoy having risen to the level of the American equivalent of the gentry class. Although the Kirk home and overall lifestyle were gentry class, he was not dismissive of or condescending to those whose intelligence levels were below his or whose standard of living was more humble. He was a true gentleman, generous and interested in others.

By this time, he had adopted a certain eccentricity of image—pork pie hat at a jaunty angle, cravat, walking stick, and an often flowery form of speech and writing rooted in past generations. This sometimes was misunderstood by those who saw him as a quaint, archaic oddity out of place in the twentieth century. Actually, although espousing traditional high principles, Kirk certainly understood the modern world and functioned well in it. The image he presented came from a sense of fun, of adventure, and, perhaps, a bit of Benjamin Disraeli's use of flamboyance as an attention grabber. George Patton too deliberately affected a flamboyant image. All of these men, however, had real substance to them. For example, Kirk's manner of speaking and writing reflected his persistent striving against the "dumbing down" of language, against those who wanted short, simple expressions of ideas, abandoning the precision and beauty of those who mastered English. In particular, among contemporaries, he admired and was influenced by T. S. Eliot.

In the 1960s, Kirk's life entered a dramatically new phase when he encountered a vivacious young coed with head-turning good looks, Annette Yvonne Cecile Courtemanche of Long Island, New York. She was a student at Molloy Catholic College for Women. He had been invited to address an event organized in opposition to Communist influence in the theatre arts. Prior to his address, she, 19 at the time, gave a talk on his recent contribution to patriotic anti-Communism, *The American Cause.* Her beauty and her mind conquered him; no longer was there a prospect for the middle-aged Kirk to finish his life a bachelor. He had written of his having had an eye for pretty girls and having dated, but there are no indications of R rated, let alone X rated, episodes in his past. She too was drawn to him. The relationship developed slowly but progressively, culminating in their marriage on September 19, 1964 and the birth of four daughters: Monica (1967), Cecilia (1968), Felicia (1970), and Andrea (1975).

The month before their marriage, he joined the Roman Catholic Church. For years he had been growing in that direction as he increasingly recognized the impossibility of having a civilization with order, justice, and freedom which did not rest on a religious foundation. In Western Civilization, this meant Christianity. As a spiritual home, Rome offered him a church which was the largest in the world and whose traditions reached back through the centuries. Although he did show appreciation for Anglicanism and Eastern Orthodoxy, he was most at home with Rome. This initially rather pragmatic position would deepen into personal Christian faith.

Politics

Although primarily warring on intellectual battlegrounds, Kirk by no means limited himself to them. A less well-known side of him was his involvement in political campaigns, on behalf of others, not himself. He had no personal political ambitions, being more oriented to the realm of ideas and aware of his limitations; with self-deprecating humor, on a number of occasions he referred to his not being tall, trimly-built, or glib of tongue. He wrote of himself that:

> Kirk's proper business was writing and speechifying. He spoke often at Washington, invited by the Department of Education, the Heritage Foundation, and other public and private sponsors, but he steered clear of political appointments, not flattering himself that he possessed the least aptitude for office. (TSI, 462)

Kirk, however, well understood that changes in thought had to be continued into the political arena in order to complete the process of reviving our civilization. Although he never met Robert A. Taft, he admired him, wrote a biography of him, and hoped for his winning the presidency in 1952. In 1964, he supported Barry Goldwater in both the primary and general election campaigns.

More dramatic was Kirk's being summoned to the White House in April 1972 by President Nixon. Back in 1967 while Nixon was an attorney in New York, the two men had met to discuss a wide range of matters, mostly foreign policy. Recently, Nixon had responded vigorously to a major North Vietnamese offensive. At this time, the Nixon policy of Vietnamization was well underway. The South Vietnamese armed forces were being increased in size and capability and taking on more of the war on land as the American Army withdrew. When this offensive started, most of our ground forces were gone. Nixon, having hoped the war would wind down as the South Vietnamese took over more of the conflict, ordered a massive increase in air strikes and soon would order the port of Haiphong closed by mines. These measures would compel the North Vietnamese to sign a treaty ending the fighting, a treaty they would ignore once Nixon was crippled by Watergate and forced from office. But, to return to April, Nixon's countermeasures led crowds of antiwar demonstrators to descend on Washington and to his being castigated by the liberal media. On April 4, Kirk and Nixon spent 40 minutes in private talking of general matters before Nixon got down to a fundamental question as to whether the United States had hope for the future. Here, it is best to let Kirk speak for himself, quoting from his memoir, *The Sword of Imagination*:

> "That depends upon public belief, Mr. President," Kirk suggested. "Despair feeds upon despair, hope upon hope. If most people believe the prophets of despair, they will seek out private hidey-holes and cease to cooperate for the common good. But if most people say, 'We are in a bad way, but we still have the resources and the intelligence and the will to work a renewal'—why, they will be roused by the exigency to common action and reform. It is all a matter of belief."

Kirk went on to offer the example of the Byzantine Empire, which—despite beginnings not altogether healthy—endured for a thousand years, experiencing alternately eras of decline and eras of reinvigoration. "No human institution lasts forever, Mr. President; but the United States is young, as great powers go; and presumably three-quarters of our existence, at least, lies before us. Our present troubles may be succeeded by an age of greatness." Such was the substance of Kirk's reply.

The President's spirits revived; he said that so he always had believed; and indeed generally he had been a sanguine politician—perhaps too sanguine. (In Washington's streets, at that hour, young persons in jeans or stranger attire were denouncing him as sanguinary, for letting Hanoi and Haiphong be bombed) (TSI, 332)

Although Kirk did not express the degree of support for Nixon that he had for Taft and Goldwater or would for Reagan, he did believe that Nixon was conservative by conviction, that his fall was more the fault of vindictive opponents and subordinates who failed him.[6]

Rather intriguing and apparently paradoxical was Kirk's support of Eugene McCarthy's quixotic independent run for the presidency in the general election of 1976. On the level of political policy there were major differences between the conservative Kirk and the liberal McCarthy. Kirk, though, had little use for either Gerald Ford or Jimmy Carter, regarding both as shallow, and did respect McCarthy as a man of integrity, depth, and as having a conservative temperament under his liberal politics. McCarthy, although disagreeing with much of *The Conservative Mind*, did write an honest critique of it and did express his admiration for Burke and de Tocqueville. There are consistent threads of thought that ran through the apparently multihued politics of Kirk, threads that will be explained in Part II.

Kirk supported Reagan, finding him a man of deeper convictions and greater ability than he initially believed. He also praised Reagan as an effective practical politician within the context of being a man of principle. This was important to Kirk who, while always keeping principle in first place, did recognize that effective governance always involves what it is possible to do, that perfection is not of this world. Reagan, in turn was familiar with Kirk, praising his writings, and having several meetings with him. Again, as with Nixon, Kirk was a guide to presidents, not a close advisor on policy issues.

Kirk also stepped into Michigan state politics, serving as a delegate to Republican state conventions and backing some candidates such as John Engler in his state senate and gubernatorial races, Joanne Emmons in her successful state senate campaigns, and my abortive attempt to win a 1980 Republican congressional nomination.

Politically, the last hurrah for Kirk was in 1992 when he supported Pat Buchanan's challenge to George H. W. Bush. Kirk had known Buchanan for years and admired him. Furthermore, Kirk, having endorsed Bush in the 1988 presidential primary battles, now was disillusioned with his administration, as will be discussed later, and actively involved himself with the Buchanan insurgency, serving as general chairman for Michigan.

As the years had rolled by, Kirk had supported himself and his family as an independent scholar, writing books, articles, and columns, editing journals, giving addresses, and being a visiting professor. His income sustained his lifestyle, but by a narrow margin, he never being a man with a good head for business. Upon his wife, Annette, fell the responsibility for maintaining solvency. He wrote 35 books, nonfiction and fiction. In the first category, several were compilations of his lectures. Among his major works, *The Conservative Mind* is the best known and, overall, the most influential. Also significant in their impact on thought are: *Enemies of the Permanent Things* (Kirk's personal favorite), *The Roots of American Order, The American Cause, The Conservative Constitution, America's British Culture,* and his biographies of Edmund Burke and T. S. Eliot. In addition, he founded and edited *Modern Age* and *The University Bookman.*

Kirk's fictional novels and short stories provided him with enjoyment, an alternative way to reach people with his ideas, and income. He wrote three full-length novels: *Old House of Fear, A Creature of the Twilight,* and *Lord of the Hollow Dark.* His numerous short stories were collected into six volumes. The content of Kirk's writings will be developed in the next section.

Evening

Kirk's physical vigor and endurance held up well into the last few years of his life. In the late 1970s he was diagnosed with diabetes, but it was controlled by dietary reform, insulin never being necessary. A mild heart attack in 1980 did not slow him down for long and his active schedule resumed. By the 1990s, though, the final slow decline began. The progressive impact of congestive heart failure was clearly evident in 1993, much weight having been melted from his progressively weakening frame. In October of that year, an impressive testimonial was held at the Dearborn Inn in Dearborn, Michigan to celebrate Kirk's 75th birthday and the 40th anniversary of the first publication of *The Conservative Mind*. To those present that night, it had all the earmarks of being the last chance to express respect, appreciation, and affection for a man who had changed the lives of so many for the better. As a Christian, his faith in eternal life was firm.

Just a few weeks prior to his death in April 1994, Kirk completed his memoir, *The Sword of Imagination*. In it, he summarized his efforts to preserve and to revitalize the essential elements of civilization—the "Permanent Things":

> Fifty-seven years have elapsed since Kirk first had drawn his literary sword and blown his literary trumpet. That Remnant he addressed had grown in numbers and earnestness; now and again it had taken a castle or a town. At the age of seventy-five Kirk could not ascertain accurately how far his exhortations had brought about such gains. What he might do to rouse others' imaginations and courage, that he had done, to the best of his limited talents. (TSI, 1995: 469)

Here is no false modesty. Kirk certainly understood that he had accomplished much, yet he also knew what lay beyond his ability. This statement was an attempt at honest evaluation within the context of Christian humility by a man who knew that the end of his days on earth was not far off. The last words of his memoir are from Shakespeare's *All's Well That Ends Well*:

> I am for the house with the narrow gate, which I take to be too little for pomp to enter: some that humble

themselves may; but many will be too chill and tender, and they "be for the flow" by way that leads to the broad gate and the great fire. (TSI, 1995: 476)

During these final weeks, for a last time, Russell, Annette, and their four daughters were together at Piety Hill. Kirk, though now weak, sleeping poorly, and eating little, visited with his family while continuing to work, indexing *Redeeming the Time* which would be published after his death. Late in the morning of April 29, he died quietly and peacefully. On the table beside his bed lay the play by Shakespeare he had read again the previous night—*All's Well That Ends Well*. How true! How appropriate for Russell Kirk!

Today, Annette continues the heritage, serving as president of The Russell Kirk Center for Cultural Renewal in Mecosta. Piety Hill remains the Kirk homestead and houses Annette's office and interns funded by the Wilbur Foundation which at one time was headed by Kirk and which continues as a significant provider of financial support for the conservative movement. It also owns four houses near Piety Hill and the Kirk library where stay people in town to work, to study, or to attend seminars. Mecosta lives on as a prime center for traditional conservatives whose roots are in Christianity.

Notes

[1] Kirk's memoir, *The Sword of Imagination*, was drawn upon extensively for this section. In addition, personal conversations with him and discussions with those who knew him well provided background and clarification.

[2] Kirk, following the pattern of others such as Henry Adams, wrote his memoir in the third person. He considered it

less egocentric, something permitting at least a degree of objectivity.

[3] Swedenborg maintained that his writings were divine revelation. In them, he recounted experiences with those no longer in this world. But, he condemned Spiritualist practices as being dangerous since evil spirits stepped into the breach when contact with those beyond this world was sought.

[4] Stoics believed that everything was part of an order which is universal and rational, that people should accept that and be impervious to pain and pleasure.

[5] The first edition was subtitled *From Burke to Santayana.* Thereafter, the subtitle was *From Burke to Eliot,* representing his maturing spiritual thought and the growing influence of the devoutly Christian Eliot.

[6] While I agree that these were factors in the fall of Nixon, I believe that his failure was more attributable to his flaws and mistakes, especially entangling himself in a web of lies over Watergate.

3

Russell Kirk's Beliefs

The Conservative Mind

Kirk's opinion concerning the likely success of the beliefs he set forth is interesting; he was a complex man, exhibiting different traits on different levels of his being. Upon meeting him, one was struck by what appeared to be an optimistic nature. He seemed to be a somewhat shy, genial man, invariably pleasant, exuding good cheer when meeting people. On a higher, intermediate level, he was less buoyant. He quoted T. S. Eliot that "As no great cause ever is wholly lost, so no great cause ever is wholly gained." He did this again toward the end of *The Sword of Imagination*, completed a matter of weeks prior to his death (TSI, 469). Setbacks are part of life; evil has strength. His initial choice of a title for *The Conservative Mind* was *The Conservative Rout*, but the publisher considered it too gloomy. Yet on the highest level, Kirk, as a Christian, was optimistic, knowing that God would triumph ultimately. This became progressively more evident in the middle and later stages of his career in both his nonfiction and fiction works.

When *The Conservative Mind* was written, Kirk's traditional conservatism was developed, but its Christian foundation was not yet fleshed out; he still was at the stage of what could be termed "civilizational Christianity," that is, he recognized the need for a good, solid civilization to have a religious foundation, but he had not yet come to a deep, personal belief in Christianity. From his youth, Kirk had demonstrated a powerful strain of traditional conservatism; his love of history and of family led him to an appreciation for community and rooted civilization. But, as a young man, he was drawn part way into the freethinking, individualistic camp as exemplified by Albert Jay Nock with whom he corresponded in the mid-1940s. Nock, however, a former Episcopal priest who had abandoned his faith, was moving in the opposite direction of Kirk who had been raised apart from settled religious convictions. Kirk, increasingly seeing that civilization must have a religious foundation, slowly was moving toward Christian belief and his traditionalist support for community and continuity were stronger than his individualism. His later vitriolic denunciation of libertarianism represented his genuine convictions and, perhaps, an annoyance with himself for having been attracted to it earlier.

With the publication of *The Conservative Mind* by Regnery in 1953, Russell Kirk, more than any other single individual, sparked the revival of conservative thought in the post-World War II world. The passing of men such as Paul Elmer More and the impact of Roosevelt's New Deal, led to rather a wasteland of serious conservative works during the 1930s and 1940s. Granted, there were some books of significance dealing with parts of the conservative message which had been published during the decade prior to 1953, books such as Friedrich A. Hayek, *The Road to Serfdom*, 1944; Richard Weaver, *Ideas Have Consequences*, 1948; and Ludwig von Mises, *Human Action*, 1949. Furthermore, in 1944, Felix Morley, William Henry Chamberlain, and Frank Hanighen had founded the journal *Human Events*. Yet, important as were these contributions, the impact of *The Conservative Mind* was far greater; the intellectual shock waves emanating from it were hard to overestimate. Conservatives now had a powerful compilation, a bringing together of rather inchoate beliefs and feelings held by many people throughout the Western World. Recent decades of liberal successes had led to discouragement, confusion, and compromise in the conservative ranks. Now, Kirk brought together the strands of traditional conservatism rooted in the Christian foundation of Western Civilization plus the pre-Christian Jewish, Greek, and Roman influences.

In this book, Kirk set forth his justly hailed six canons of conservative thought. It should be noted that while he enunciated fundamental values, throughout his career he consistently opposed a rigid systemization of conservatism. His belief in individual thought and creativity were too strong for him to want any conservative equivalent of Marxist orthodoxy. Yet, he did realize that there had to be clear principles that characterize the movement and draw people together. This is an apparent contradiction, but it is an achievable balance, one which he explained carefully. Somewhat concised, the canons are as follows:

1. Belief in a transcendent order, or body of natural law, which rules society as well as conscience. Political problems, at bottom, are religious and moral problems.
2. Affection for the proliferating variety and mystery of human existence, as opposed to the narrowing uniformity, egalitarianism, and utilitarian aims of most radical systems...
3. Conviction that civilized society requires orders and classes, as against the notion of a "classless society".... If

natural distinctions are effaced among men, oligarchs fill the vacuum. Ultimate equality in the judgment of God, and equality before courts of law, are recognized by conservatives; but equality of condition, they think, means equality in servitude and boredom.

4. Persuasion that freedom and property are closely linked.... Economic leveling, they maintain, is not economic progress.

5. Faith in prescription and distrust of "sophisters, calculators, and economists" who would reconstruct society upon abstract designs. Custom, convention, and old prescription are checks both upon man's anarchic impulse and upon the innovator's lust for power.

6. Recognition that change may not be salutary reform: hasty innovation may be a devouring conflagration, rather than a torch of progress. Society must alter, for prudent change is the means of progress... (TCM, 8–9).

Throughout over 40 more years of writing, Kirk would develop and elaborate his beliefs, but everything would be within the context of these canons. His religious faith would grow and deepen substantially, but canon one already was his conviction in 1952 when *The Conservative Mind* was finished. Canon five set forth his devotion to tradition, but numbers two and six made clear that people are to be free from enforced conformity and that prudent change is essential to civilizational survival. Societal order and stability were affirmed in numbers three and four.

Later, perhaps wanting to avoid canonization of these six points, Kirk set forth ten principles of conservative thought, published in *The Politics of Prudence* which came out in 1993. Essentially the same ideas are in both. Kirk continued to recognize the need for a body of unifying principles while recoiling at any hint of enforced orthodoxy. (POP, 17–25) Because *The Conservative Mind* is more widely read, the six canons will continue to be more influential than the ten principles, although the latter are being disseminated on the internet.[1] Also somewhat concised, the ten conservative principles he discussed are:

1. First, the conservative believes that there exists an enduring moral order. That order is made for man, and man is made for it: human nature is a constant, and moral truths are permanent.
   This word order signifies harmony. There are two aspects or types of order: the inner order of the soul, and the outer order of the commonwealth.

2. Second, the conservative adheres to custom, convention, and continuity. It is old custom that enables people to live together peaceably; the destroyers of custom demolish more than they know or desire. It is through convention—a word much abused in our time—that we contrive to avoid perpetual disputes about rights and duties: law at base is a body of conventions. Continuity is the means of linking generation to generation; it matters as much for society as it does for the individual; without it, life is meaningless. When successful revolutionaries have effaced old customs, derided old conventions, and broken the continuity of social institutions—why, presently they discover the necessity of establishing fresh customs, conventions, and continuity; but that process is painful and slow; and the new social order that eventually emerges may be much inferior to the old order that radicals overthrew in their zeal for the Earthly Paradise.

3. Third, conservatives believe in what may be called the principle of prescription. Conservatives sense that modern people are dwarfs on the shoulders of giants, able to see farther than their ancestors only because of the great stature of those who have preceded us in time. Therefore conservatives very often emphasize the importance of prescription—that is, of things established by immemorial usage, so that the mind of man runneth not to the contrary. There exist rights of which the chief sanction is their antiquity—including rights to property, often. Similarly, our morals are prescriptive in great part. Conservatives argue that we are unlikely, we moderns, to make any brave new discoveries in morals or politics or taste. It is perilous to weigh every passing issue on the basis of private judgment and private rationality. The individual is foolish, but the species is wise, Burke declared.

4. Fourth, conservatives are guided by their principle of prudence. Burke agrees with Plato that in the statesman, prudence is chief among virtues. Any public measure ought to be judged by its probable long-term consequences, not merely by temporary advantage or popularity.... The conservative declares that he acts only after sufficient reflection, having weighed the consequences. Sudden and slashing reforms are as perilous as sudden and slashing surgery.

5. Fifth, conservatives pay attention to the principle of variety. They feel affection for the proliferating intricacy of long-established social institutions and modes of life, as distinguished from the narrowing uniformity and deadening egalitarianism of radical systems. For the preservation of a healthy diversity in any civilization, there must survive orders and classes, differences in material

condition, and many sorts of inequality. The only true forms of equality are equality at the Last Judgment and equality before a just court of law; all other attempts at leveling must lead, at best, to social stagnation.

6. Sixth, conservatives are chastened by their principle of imperfectability. Human nature suffers irremediably from certain grave faults, the conservatives know. Man being imperfect, no perfect social order ever can be created. To seek for utopia is to end in disaster, the conservative says: we are not made for perfect things. All that we reasonably can expect is a tolerably ordered, just, and free society in which some evils, maladjustments, and suffering will continue to lurk. By proper attention to prudent reform, we may preserve and improve this tolerable order.

7. Seventh, conservatives are persuaded that freedom and property are closely linked. Separate property from private possession, and Leviathan becomes master of all. Upon the foundation of private property, great civilizations are built. The more widespread is the possession of private property, the more stable and productive is a commonwealth. Economic leveling, conservatives, maintain, is not economic progress. Getting and spending are not the chief aims of human existence; but a sound economic basis for the person, the family, and the commonwealth is much to be desired.

8. Eighth, conservatives uphold voluntary community, quite as they oppose involuntary collectivism. Although Americans have been attached strongly to privacy and private rights, they also have been a people conspicuous for a successful spirit of community.... Whatever is beneficent and prudent in modern democracy is made possible through cooperative

volition. If, then, in the name of an abstract Democracy, the functions of community are transferred to distant political direction—why, real government by the consent of the governed gives way to a standardizing process hostile to freedom and human dignity.

9. Ninth, the conservative perceives the need for prudent restraints upon power and upon human passions. Politically speaking, power is the ability to do as one likes, regardless of the wills of one's fellows. A state in which an individual or a small group is able to dominate the wills of their fellows without check is a despotism, whether it is called monarchical or aristocratic or democratic.

Constitutional restrictions, political checks and balances, adequate enforcement of the laws, the old intricate web of restraints upon will and appetite—these, the conservative approves as instruments of freedom and order. A just government maintains a healthy tension between the claims of authority and the claims of liberty.

10. Tenth, the thinking conservative understands that permanence and change must be recognized and reconciled in a vigorous society. The conservative knows that any healthy society is influenced by two forces, which Samuel Taylor Coleridge called its Permanence and its Progression. The Permanence of a society is formed by those enduring interests and convictions that give us stability and continuity; without that Permanence, the fountains of the great deep are broken up, society slipping into anarchy. The Progression in a society is that spirit and that body of talents which urge us on to prudent reform and improvement; without that Progression, a people stagnate.

Therefore the intelligent conservative endeavors to reconcile the claims of Permanence and the claims of Progression.

As can be seen, the ten principles do not clash with the six canons, although the former are much more developed, eight pages being devoted to them in *The Politics of Prudence* whereas the six canons occupied just over one page in *The Conservative Mind.* For example, canon five was expressed in principles two and four and principles six and eight were implied in the canons, but not stated as explicitly.

It was Kirk's conviction that at various times and under varying circumstances conservatives will emphasize certain of these principles more than others, but, taken together, they provide a useful summary of what has characterized modern conservative thought over the past two centuries.

Intellectual Influences

Much can be learned about any individual by examining the people he or she most admires. So it is with Russell Kirk. Discussed here are four persons he looked to as his intellectual development progressed. In two instances, John Adams and Orestes Brownson, he was influential in reintroducing them to mid-twentieth-century audiences. It must be noted that Kirk was a deep, independent thinker rather than a mirror who reflected images or a blotter who merely absorbed the ideas of others. He identified key minds, distilled their beliefs, wove the thread which connected them, and added his own contributions to the revival of traditional conservatism in the post-World War II West.

Edmund Burke

Of all the prominent British and American[2] contributors of modern conservative philosophy discussed by Kirk in *The Conservative Mind*, Edmund Burke came first both chronologically and in significance. The French Revolution of 1789 unleashed on Western Civilization radical forces which struck at the very roots of that civilization; Christianity was rejected and traditional forms of government were not reformed, but rather destroyed. Out of this came chaos, then dictatorship. Americans such as George Washington, John Adams, John Jay, and Alexander Hamilton recognized the danger, but Burke was first off the mark with a major work, his 1790 *Reflections on the Revolution in France*.

Burke was born in Ireland in 1729, the son of a Church of Ireland (Anglican) father who was a prominent attorney, and a Roman Catholic mother. He was educated at Trinity College, Dublin, receiving his Bachelor of Arts degree in 1748. In the spring of 1750, he crossed the Irish Sea to study law at the Middle Temple in London. Losing interest in becoming an attorney, he moved for a while in literary circles, then entered the political arena as secretary to Lord Rockingham, leader of the Whig Party and sometime prime minister, more often leader of the opposition. Burke later served in the House of Commons and held middle level government appointments. His real significance, though, was as the intellectual leader of the Whig cause. As an aside, it is interesting to note that when discussing Burke in *The Conservative Mind*, Kirk described what it was to be a Whig in ways that, allowing for differences in time and place, were intriguingly evocative of Kirk himself: "The Whigs were opponents of arbitrary monarchical power, advocates of the internal reform of administration, men generally dubious of England's ventures abroad." (TCM, 14)

The above words certainly described Burke. As the starting point for his philosophy, he was a Christian. He sharply disagreed with the social contract theory of John Locke who saw the state owing its origin to the determination of human beings to enter into a contract agreed upon by them. Burke went deeper, believing that the real contract was with God. As is taught in Romans 13, God created the state; people govern themselves within the context of His will. Burke by no means was a creature of the eighteenth-century Enlightenment.

In addition to being a Christian, he was a traditionalist. Traditions can be wrong and are subject to change, but in a civilized society it must be prudent change within a context of order and justice. Anything which is a tradition must have been supported by a large number of people for a long time. Unless found contrary to God's revealed will, tradition should be given the benefit of the doubt and altered only with care lest the framework of civilization be shattered. Attempts to achieve perfection in this world through human action lead to chaos and to restore order, dictatorship ensues. So Burke and Kirk learned through their study of history. In his biography, *Edmund Burke: A Genius Reconsidered*, Kirk stated:

> But Utopia never will be found here below, Burke knew: politics is the art of the possible, not of perfectibility. We never will be as gods. Improvement is the work of slow exploration and persuasion, never unfixing old interests at once. Mere sweeping innovation is not reform. Once immemorial moral habits are broken by the rash Utopian, once the old checks upon will and appetite are

discarded, the inescapable sinfulness of human nature asserts itself: and those who aspired to usurp the throne of God find that they have contrived a terrestrial Hell. (EB, 166)

This brilliantly encapsulated the conservative philosophy of Edmund Burke, Russell Kirk, and multitudes of others who have striven to be both exalted in thought and practical in act.

Prior to the outbreak of fighting, Burke supported the American colonists in their opposition to the arbitrary rule of George III and his government, an arbitrariness demonstrated by the Stamp Act of 1765. Parliament, he believed, should not directly tax the colonies, but depend on voluntary grants for the common defense from the colonial legislatures, at least one house of which was elected. His hope was for an empire joined together by common principles. As a loyal subject of the crown and one opposed to revolutionary change, Burke did not back the colonists during the war, but did work for an end to the conflict with as little bitterness engendered as possible.

Burke opposed the idea of democracy based on universal suffrage. His concept of what was right was not based on numbers, but rather on higher determinants—God's revelation and natural law. Within these limits, government should be with the consent of the governed. But, who are the governed who will make the decisions? Burke believed in a franchise limited by considerations of achievement rather than being a right bestowed on those who simply have managed to live a certain number of years. In *The Conservative Mind,* Kirk wrote of Burke's belief that there were general criteria for voting such as moral character, property, and education, but that no precise formula existed, that "the extent of the franchise was a question to be determined by prudence and experience, varying with the character of the age." (TCM, 19) Human beings, contrary to the teachings of Jean Jacques Rousseau, do not determine what is true and what is good. Between Burke and Rousseau, two men of the eighteenth century, a vast chasm opened, a chasm still separating their disciples in the ongoing struggle for Western Civilization. As Kirk summarized it:

The Age of Rousseau: the era of abstraction, feeling, emancipation, expansion, equality, the people absolute, the kiss bestowed upon the universe, the deity impotent. The system of Burke: prescription, experience, duty, old ties, social gradation, the reign of law, the love engendered by association, the Author of our being omnipotent. (EB, 8)

The choice was, and still is, between radicalism separated from God and traditional Western Civilization rooted in God. Both Burke and Kirk regarded the study of history as essential to comprehend the present and to prepare for the future. History, they saw as the record of providence at work.

John Adams

The second individual discussed by Kirk in *The Conservative Mind* was John Adams, over the past two decades the subject of several excellent biographies, especially David McCullough's Pulitzer Prize winning *John Adams*. Other biographers of note include Joseph Ellis and John Ferling. To a significant extent, however, when Kirk here wrote of

Adams (*The Conservative Mind* was completed in 1952), he had slipped into obscurity, remembered as having held office between Washington and Jefferson, but for little else. Kirk was responsible for reviving interest in this admirable and interesting man, writing of him that "His learning and his courage made him great, and he became the founder of true conservatism in America." (TCM, 71)

Adams was born on October 30, 1735, in what today is Quincy, Massachusetts, into a solidly middle-class family. Graduating from Harvard in 1755, he became an attorney and started his rise in politics.

He was elected to the Continental Congress in 1774. Interestingly, Congress gave the flinty, sometimes vain and petty Adams, diplomatic assignments in Europe where he served the cause effectively in the Netherlands, in France, and, after peace, in Britain. His virtues of integrity, dedication to his country, intelligence, courage, and work ethic far outweighed his defects. He served two terms as vice president under Washington before defeating Jefferson for the presidency in 1796. In 1800, in a rematch, Jefferson won a narrow victory.

John Adams was one of the most influential of the founders. His work as a writer setting forth the case for American independence and arguing for the foundational principles and form of government for the new country were vital. Especially important were his *Thoughts on Government, A Defense of the Constitutions of Government of the United States,* and *Discourses on Davila.* Although *The Federalist,* written by Alexander Hamilton, James Madison, and John Jay, rightly considered a classic in political thought, is better known than anything written by Adams, his works were impressive and deserve more attention. Commenting on the writings of Adams, Kirk wrote that "Taken all in all, this body of political thought exceeds, both in bulk and in penetration, any other work on government by an American." (TCM, 87–88) Specifically, *A Defense of the Constitutions* he referred to as "the most thorough treatise on political institutions ever produced in the United States." (TCM, 101) Adams believed in mixed government, that to have stability and freedom it is essential to balance the monarchical, aristocratic, and democratic principles. These were established in the United States Constitution. The office of president secured the first. The Senate, chosen by state legislatures for 6-year terms, reflected the aristocratic principle and the House of Representatives elected directly by the voters for 2-year terms, brought in the democratic element. Adams opposed having absolute power in the hands of any one of these; mixed government was the best way to maximize the potentiality for good and to minimize the prospects for evil. The negative aspects of human nature, such as the desire for power, for personal aggrandizement, would be controlled and channeled as well as could be done by human planning. It should be noted that to Adams, aristocracy meant natural aristocracy, that is, one based on individual capabilities as key rather than being determined by birth. He consistently affirmed that people of ability should be able to rise without being inhibited by the majority and that the mass of people should not be oppressed by the talented few. He understood, clearly, human nature and both the possibilities and the limitations of human government.

Orestes Brownson

Another thinker of note whose influence on Kirk was significant was Orestes Brownson, a nineteenth-century

American who wandered through a number of religions
before ending up a devout Roman Catholic. Raised a
Calvinist Congregationalist in New England, he subsequently was Presbyterian, Universalist, and Unitarian,[3] in
which denomination he was ordained. He later founded
and led his own group, the Society for Christian Union
and Progress. Yet, nowhere did he find a sense of God's
true presence and, consequently, of security and peace.
He came to believe that humankind needed divine grace
through the true church and that this meant becoming
a Roman Catholic. A liberal politically as well during this
period of his life, Brownson's disappointment with the
defeat of the Democratic Party in the election of 1840
resulted in his disillusionment with majoritarian democracy and started his migration to conservative political
philosophy.

A well-known and widely respected figure in the nineteenth century, Brownson had faded almost to oblivion
before being reintroduced to the thinking public by Kirk.
A solid conservative by his middle years, Brownson articulated much the same message as Kirk, although Kirk had
a more difficult task in the latter half of the twentieth century as he labored to reinvigorate the principles in which
they both believed. Under God, the will of the people
should prevail in society. But, as Kirk pointed out, all too
often those first two words are pushed aside.

In his best known book, *The American Republic*, published
in 1865, Brownson set forth his conviction that every nation
has been chosen by God to fulfill a particular destiny:

> The Jews were the chosen people of God, through
> whom the primitive traditions were to be preserved
> in their purity and integrity, and the Messiah was to

come. The Greeks were the chosen people of God, for the development and realization of the beautiful or the divine splendor in art, and of the true in science and philosophy; and the Romans, for the development of the state, law, and jurisprudence. (Brownson, 2003, 2–3)

The destiny of the United States, he averred, was to continue the work of Greece and Rome, indeed, to surpass them both. We should rival Greece in art and outdo it in science and philosophy. Brownson further stated that this country was to assume the mantle of Rome and go beyond to reconcile law and liberty, the authority of the state with the freedom of the individual. The Greeks and Roman asserted the power of the state excessively against individual freedom. Modern countries, he said, either do the same or weaken the state with too much individualism. Again, the American mission is to harmonize what all too often are forces in conflict (Brownson, 2003, 3).

Kirk and Brownson had, as did Edmund Burke, a thorough understanding of history resting on a firmly Christian foundation which led them to traditional conservative affirmations.

T. S. Eliot

Kirk's relationship with T. S. Eliot, an older contemporary, was one of mutual respect and personal friendship. He wrote an excellent and well-received biography of Eliot. As was mentioned earlier, Kirk's favorite of all his works was *Enemies of the Permanent Things*. Although Kirk may have preferred this book, it is not the one for which he is best known, ranking behind *The Conservative Mind, The Roots*

of American Order, and, perhaps, a couple of others. It is
ironic that often the works most favored by their creators
were not so regarded by the market. The term "permanent things" he derived from Eliot who used it to mean
those abiding verities from God which, therefore, do not
depend on human sanction for their validity.

Eliot was born in St. Louis, Missouri in 1888 and earned
his bachelor's and master's degrees from Harvard before
spending a year in Paris at the Sorbonne. He then studied a year at Merton College, Oxford prior to his serving
as a lecturer at Birbeck College, University of London. In
1916, he submitted his Ph.D. dissertation to Harvard, but
it was not awarded to him since he did not appear in person to defend it. He continued to teach, was a banker for
a period of time, then joined the publishing firm of Faber
and Gwyer, later Faber and Faber where he remained for
the rest of his career.

Primarily known as a literary figure, Kirk was not alone in
considering him the greatest twentieth-century poet, Eliot
also wrote on world affairs and on politics from the vantage point of a Christian traditionalist. In *The Conservative
Mind*, Kirk quoted from Eliot's great play *Murder in the
Cathedral* that:

> Those who put their faith in worldly order
> Not controlled by the order of God,
> In confident ignorance, but arrest disorder
> Make it fast, breed fatal disease,
> Degrade what they exalt. (TCM, 466)

Consistent with that affirmation, Eliot vehemently rejected
both Communism and Fascism as attacks on Christian civilization. On this point, Kirk quoted from Eliot's *The Idea*

of a Christian Society that "If you will not have God (and He is a jealous God) you should pay your respects to Hitler or Stalin." (POP, 86)

Eliot lamented the separation of political thought and political action, that all too frequently serious thinkers do not enter the political arena and that those in the arena do not think deeply. This, of course, is not unusual when democracy is combined with universal suffrage. Between the two extremes referred to above by Eliot, there should be gradations. Eliot himself was little involved, Kirk rather more. Eliot did assert the necessity for the taking of principled stands apart from considerations of political gain or discouragement. He wrote that:

> There should always be a few writers preoccupied in penetrating to the core of the matter, in trying to arrive at the truth and to set it forth, without too much hope, without ambition to alter the immediate course of affairs and without being downcast or defeated when nothing appears to ensue. (POP, 83)

This would tie in with the observation by Lee Edwards in *The Conservative Revolution: The Movement that Remade America* that three levels of conservative activists were responsible for the conservative revival in this country. First came the thinkers, who made the philosophical case. Second were the popularizers, those who presented the philosophical case so that it could be understood by the average person. Then came the political leaders who implemented public policy based on these conservative principles. It all begins, though, with the thinkers without whom there is nothing to popularize and no foundation under public policy.

Although Eliot had proclaimed himself an Anglo-Catholic in religion, a classicist in literature, and a royalist in politics, he and Kirk were very close in thought. Had Kirk been English, he no doubt likewise would have designated himself a royalist, proclaiming the advantages of monarchy as a repository of tradition, as a system deeply rooted in the history of the country. This statement was written in the preface of *For Launcelot Andrewes* which was published in 1928. Eliot believed in constitutional monarchy, rejecting the more absolutist monarchical views of, for example, Joseph de Maistre. He valued monarchy as a repository of tradition and as a source of unity transcending changes in political leadership. The growing political turmoil in much of Europe during the 1920s increased Eliot's focus on legitimacy, continuity, and stability (EAHA, 144–145). Perhaps too, Kirk would have been an Anglo-Catholic. At any rate, in terms of civilizational principles, the two were in accord. Near the end of *Eliot and His Age*, Kirk summed up the contribution of Eliot to our civilization:

> As a critic of society, he had stripped the follies of the time. He had not spared the morals of his age, or its politics, or its economics, or its notions of education, or its strange gods. He had striven to renew modern man's understanding of the norms of order and justice and freedom, in the person and in the commonwealth. He had not offered the opiate of ideology[4]: he had pleaded for a return to enduring principle, and for recognition of the tensions which are necessary to a tolerable civil social order.... The alternative to a totalist order, a social life-in-death, an existence without culture or freedom—so he had told those who would listen—is a social order founded upon religious truth. (EAHA, 417)

Of course, it could be observed that these words also encapsulate the mission of Russell Kirk.

Christopher Dawson

These four individuals were discussed extensively in *The Conservative Mind*, published in 1953; they remained significant interests of and influences on Kirk. A fifth man, Christopher Dawson, is intriguing because his effect on Kirk grew as Kirk's Christianity became a bigger and bigger part of his life.[5] Dawson (1889–1970) was raised in Yorkshire and educated at Oxford. He converted from Anglo-Catholicism to Roman Catholicism in 1914. A devout believer, he rejected the argument that the Middle Ages in Western Civilization were a sterile period of limited significance. Countering this, Dawson wrote extensively that these were the years of the formulation and rise of Western Civilization and that the Catholic Church was the key factor in this development. By the 1920s and 1930s, he became one of the significant thinkers in the West, an important influence on T. S. Eliot and J. R. R. Tolkien. From 1958–1962, he held the Chauncey Stillman Chair of Roman Catholic Studies at Harvard.

Increasingly, the way of thinking represented by Dawson was foundational with Kirk. In *The Sword of Imagination*, he referred to Dawson's impact on his viewing of civilization as grounded on that which comes from above and beyond this world. Dawson, he wrote, saw with clarity that "a civilization cannot long survive the dying of belief in a transcendent order that brought the culture into being." (TSI, 474)

Kirk made reference to Dawson's *Religion and Culture* in which he warned of the crisis in Western Civilization as the drift from Christianity proceeded. As Kirk quoted him:

> There is an absolute limit to the progress that can be achieved by the perfectionment of scientific techniques detached from spiritual aims and moral values.... The recovery of moral control and the return to spiritual order have become the indispensable conditions of human survival. But they can be achieved only by a profound change in the spirit of modern civilization. (RTT, 12)

Dawson went on to call for reestablishing the close link between Christianity and culture.

Had Kirk been granted a few more years of life in this world, he would have undertaken the editing of Dawson's works, reintroducing him to the reading public as another facet of Kirk's crusade to reinvigorate the Christian roots of Western Civilization.

Education

At the forefront of Kirk's myriads of interests was education, what was wrong with it and how it could be changed for the better. He wrote three books on the matter,[6] discussed it in other works, spoke on it, and wrote articles setting forth his views. His disgust with declining standards was expressed in his writing of his undergraduate days at Michigan State and of the time he spent there after World War II as a member of the faculty. Key considerations which created and fed this decline were discussed by Kirk.

First, there developed slowly but progressively a move
to de-Christianize institutions of higher learning, turning
away from the belief that there are objective truths on
which civilization is based. In the nineteenth century the
influence of John Dewey grew, fueling this secularization
and bringing in a stronger element of egalitarianism, of
democratization. In order to have an increasing number
of people attending colleges and universities, standards
had to be lowered. This change was not seen merely as
useful, but was considered a positive good. Of course,
more students meant more revenue and more influence
as these institutions often grew to immense size, becoming progressively more impersonal and less impressive
intellectually. An interesting commentary of the trend
in higher education is to consider John Jay who entered
Kings College, later Columbia University, at the age of
14. In order to be admitted, among other things, he had
to demonstrate competence in both Greek and Latin.
One requirement was to translate the first ten chapters
of the Gospel of John from Greek into Latin. It is one
thing to raise people up to meet standards, but lowering
standards in order to increase numbers is a totally different matter.

Kirk also lamented that all too often teachers come
from the lower rungs of high school and college students.
Furthermore, too little attention was devoted to educating
teachers in the subjects they would teach while too much
time was given to mind-numbing education, how-to-teach
courses.

Another complaint by Kirk was that colleges and universities have become too get-a-job oriented to the detriment
of higher matters. Certainly graduates seek employment;
that is nothing new since for generations these institutions

had been producing professional people who had successful careers. This, though, was secondary to what was their
primary purpose.[7] Kirk further said of colleges and universities that:

> They ought to be centers for genuinely humane and
> genuinely scientific studies, attended by young peo-
> ple of healthy intellectual curiosity who actually show
> some interest in mind and conscience. I am saying
> that the higher learning is meant to develop order
> in the soul, for the human person's own sake. I am
> saying that the higher learning is meant to develop
> order in the commonwealth, for the republic's sake.
> I am arguing that a system of higher education which
> has forgotten these ends is decadent; but that decay
> may be arrested, and that reform and renewal still are
> conceivable. (WMK, 83)

That last point is significant because Kirk did not simply gnash his teeth and bewail what had happened to
education; he believed that change for the better was
possible and had a number of specific improvements.
He believed that renewal should be based on private
institutions which are grounded in Christianity. (DAR,
294) In *Enemies of the Permanent Things*, Kirk wrote that
"The Church is that great repository of authoritative wisdom; so real education necessarily is religious; 'secular-
ized' instruction undoes itself." (EPT, 59) He regarded
favorably such Roman Catholic institutions as Thomas
Aquinas College and Christendom College, as well as
Grove City College (Presbyterian) and Hillsdale College
(originally Baptist). There were others which he opined
had preserved much of their character and still were

good centers for genuine learning: William and Mary, Louisiana State, Pepperdine, and Vanderbilt. Also, as discussed in the preface, he was impressed with the idea behind International College and its manner of operation, so reminiscent of his experiences with independent study and meetings with the professor to whom he was assigned.

Kirk argued that colleges should be gender separate so as to avoid distractions in academic activities. Since, though, he was family oriented, he advocated having these separate colleges in proximity to each other permitting socialization which he certainly favored (DAR, 306).

Kirk also set forth his conviction that there should not be a multitude of courses, but rather a smaller number with more depth. The academic year should be 6 months in length to permit independent study and travel. There would be 1 month off at Christmas, one at Easter plus summer. Also, undergraduate degrees should be awarded after 3 years with, perhaps, a fourth year in order to earn an honors degree (DAR, 302–303).

Kirk summed up the purpose of higher education with the teaching that "Universities were founded to sustain faith by reason—and to maintain order in the soul and in the commonwealth." (WMK, 101) Education is good, but separated from moral principles rooted in the revelation of God, it is, at best, of limited use in improving society; at worst, it is then a destructive force.

Economics

No doubt the words "polymath" and "Renaissance man" do get used freely and casually, but, in the case of Russell

Kirk they are most apt. Among his less known areas of
intellectual endeavor is economics. He did integrate economics into his major works, such as *The Conservative Mind.*
In canon four of the six canons of conservative thought,
Kirk linked freedom and private property and opposed
economic leveling by government (TCM, 9). On numerous occasions, both in print and in speeches, he affirmed
his support for a private sector economy, not one run by
the government. He credited the teachings set forth in
Adam Smith's *Wealth of Nations* (full title, *An Inquiry Into
the Nature and Causes of the Wealth of Nations*) with providing
the philosophical underpinnings of the economic prosperity of the United Kingdom and of the United States. He
also made the interesting point that Smith's thought was
drawn upon by both Secretary of the Treasury Alexander
Hamilton and by those who opposed his policies, pointing
to the widespread influence of Smith on both sides of the
Atlantic (RTT, 266).

But, Kirk was firm in his opposition to making economics the key factor in civilization; he had no use for economic determinism whether from the left or the right.
Market economics are good, but not the source of good.
Economics is always discussed by Kirk as part of a broader
framework. Civilization rests ultimately on spiritual principles derived from revelation and tradition. Within this
context, market economic forces are beneficial in promoting freedom.

Kirk, as is true of everyone, revealed much about himself by writing of those with whom he agreed. Wilhelm
Roepke was one. Kirk's admiration for him is very evident to anyone who reads the chapter on Roepke in *The
Politics of Prudence.* He was a German economist who was
born in 1899 and died in 1966. A decorated veteran of the

German army in World War I, he later ran afoul of Hitler's regime, lost his teaching position, and went into exile in Switzerland. A devout Christian, Roepke opposed Marxist and Nazi command economies as well as laissez-faire absolutism. He believed in a decentralized market economy rooted in family and community. These convictions he developed in his books, such as *The Social Crisis of Our Time*, *Economics of the Free Society*, and *A Humane Economy*. But, the discussion of economics as part of other works is not all there is to it. In addition, Kirk was commissioned by the Educational Research Council of America to write an economics textbook for high school students. He did so and *Economics: Work and Prosperity*, was published in 1989. He tempered his style somewhat, taking into account the target audience, but not too much; it still distinctively is a Kirk book. He did not fall into the all too common trap of writing down to the students. This book does provide the technical economics material that must be learned by any student of the subject, but enlivens such rather dry topics as "diminishing marginal utility" with illustrations, some historical, some from his imagination.

Kirk extolled the virtues of an economy free from government domination: "In a market economy, healthy competition improves the quality of goods and lowers their prices.... This healthy competition in the selling of goods is a major reason why countries with a market economy are prosperous." (EWP, 121) Also, this thriving economy makes possible private generosity (EWP, 368). There is, though, a broader context. Kirk pointed out that economic motives do account for much of the way people act, but do not explain everything about human actions; we are more complex than simply being economic creatures.

No libertarian he, Kirk did allow for some restrictions
to be imposed by the government to protect the public
from things which are inherently dangerous by either for-
bidding them or regulating them. Monopolies are one
example (EWP, 16, 139). The government does have a
role, preserving life, liberty, and property, providing an
environment within which market economics can work.
As he stated: "A sound economy cannot exist without a
political state to protect it. Foolish political interference
with the economy can result in general poverty, but wise
political encouragement of the economy helps a society
toward prosperity." (EWP, 365)

Moving to more foundational matters, Kirk was firm in
his assertion that an economy cannot function effectively
without a set of moral principles accepted by most of the
people (EWP, 365). These principles rise out of a Biblical
foundation. For example, Kirk presented the Parable
of the Talents as recorded in Matthew 25:15–30. In it,
Christ taught that a rich man who was going on a journey
entrusted different sums of money to three of his servants,
the amount depending on the ability of each individual.
When he returned, he learned that two had increased the
value of what had been entrusted to them while the third
had done nothing. The two were praised, the other was
condemned. Kirk stated that the purpose of the parable
was to teach that people were to make good use of their
time on earth, that is, they were to develop themselves as
good stewards in the service of God. Frequently, Christ
used parables to convey His points. Here He used a capi-
talistic example. Not only are the points He is making true,
but the means used to present them also must be true.

Three final quotations from this text encapsulate Kirk's
view concerning the limited scope of economics and the

overarching principles to which it and everything else are subordinate:

> Economics is not a religion. Nor is it a political system. Nor is it a sure recipe for happiness. Economics is simply the study of producing, distributing, and consuming goods. (EWP, 39)
> Money can buy a great many things—perhaps more things than it should. But it cannot buy good character, or honor, or the love of created beings—or the love of God. (EWP, 222)
> In the industrially developed nations of our time, a great many people think they will be happy if only they obtain plenty of goods and services. Christians know this is not true, however. The Bible teaches that happiness comes from being in God's will. (EWP, 266)

There is nothing revolutionary in Kirk's thought. What he has called for is market economics conducted ethically within the fold of a civilization rooted in Christianity. There is more depth here than in the standard study in this field, a book which is limited to the consideration of economics only. For example, in *Free to Choose*, Milton and Rose Friedman wrote that "The combination of economic and political freedom produced a golden age in both Great Britain and the United States in the nineteenth century." (Friedman and Friedman: 1980, 3) This statement is true as far as it goes, but it is not as thorough as is the Kirk presentation.

As conservatism grew stronger philosophically and politically and as liberalism waned, the differences between those who rejected the old liberal establishment became more pronounced. Two movements in particular shared

Kirk's rejection of liberalism, but deviated from his traditional conservatism in terms of both foundational beliefs and policy stands.

Libertarianism

Already in the 1950s the conservative movement was being torn between traditional conservatives and libertarians. Both valued principled, free societies, but differed sharply concerning how to build them. Libertarians believed that freedom must come first, that then justice and order could be established. To Kirk, this was nonsense. He averred that only when order had been secured could justice and freedom emerge and thrive. If freedom is exalted as primary, then justice and order will not follow; chaos and societal breakdown instead will ensue and despotism will fill the vacuum. Libertarian beliefs are unrealistic and, ultimately, destructive to civilization. Kirk was definite in wanting all three—order, justice, and freedom—but was clear in espousing order as the essential first.

Frank Meyer labored vigorously to bring about a coming together, a "fusion" it came to be called, of the traditionalists and the libertarians into one conservative camp, bringing together the love of "the permanent things" of the former and the orientation to freedom as the ultimate good proclaimed by the latter. In his biography of Kirk, James Person set forth his belief that this even attracted Kirk, who, said Person, shared much in common with Meyer, that by the latter stages of their lives "Kirk and Meyer had far more bridges than walls between them." (Person, 1999: 194) Meyer did become a Roman Catholic shortly before his death, so they did have that in common.

Had Meyer lived longer, maybe his theology would have affected his philosophy. That we cannot know in this world. Kirk continued to be leery of Meyer's thought. Of himself, he wrote that "He was ill at ease with Willmore Kendall, a Rousseauistic populist; and with Frank Meyer, a former Communist who had transferred his zeal to something called Fusionism." (TSI, 188) Kirk's being ill at ease was understandable; in a *Freeman* review, Meyer condemned *The Conservative Mind* as "collectivism rebaptized." Kirk said of him "An extreme individualist, Meyer suspected Kirk of being a Trojan Horse within the conservative camp." (TSI, 150) Prospects for fusion at best were slim.

In *The Sword of Imagination*,[8] Kirk summed up his rejection of libertarianism as fuzzy in thinking and ineffective in acting:

> Many libertarians thought Soviet Russia no real menace: free trade and cordial handshakes would work happy conciliation; they would sweep away the state almost wholly, or perhaps altogether, as Marx aspired to. Somehow enlightened self-interest would cure all the ills to which flesh was heir. These groups constituted merely what T. S. Eliot called "a chirping sect," petty political sectaries of the sort Burke pictured as "the insects of the hour," noisy as they were ineffectual, ideological cliques forever splitting into sects still smaller and odder, but rarely conjugating. (TSI, 144)

Kirk's rejection of libertarian beliefs never flagged. In his 1981 lecture for the Heritage Foundation entitled "Libertarians: Chirping Sectaries," he dismissed the idea of fusion, stating that "To talk of forming a league or coalition between these two is like advocating a union of

ice and fire." (RTT, 271) He further charged that "The
perennial libertarian, like Satan, can bear no authority
temporal or spiritual." (RTT, 28) Kirk was convinced that
the libertarian enthronement of freedom as the highest
good was wrong and dangerous. Certainly he believed in
freedom, but it must operate within the context of God's
order.

To illustrate this, Kirk discussed G. K. Chesterton's
short story "The Yellow Bird" in which Professor Ivanov,
who opposed all limitations and exalted the absolute
removal of restraints, carried out his convictions by freeing a canary from its cage only to have it unable to survive
in the forest where it was killed and the professor also
smashed a goldfish bowl to free its residents (POP, 163–
164). His point was clear that we operate within a framework and that to remove this is destructive. Conservatives,
Kirk averred, understand that true freedom is found only
in service to God, an apparent paradox, but perfectly
clear to believers.

Neoconservatism

During the 1980s, a new classification came into prominence—neoconservatism. Typically, neoconservatives had
been Democrats who stayed within the party of Harry
Truman, but found themselves alienated from that party
as during the 1960s it became less firm in its opposition
to Soviet imperialism, surged to bigger government and
more egalitarianism under Lyndon Johnson, supported
more moral permissiveness as a reaction to the culture
conflicts of the 1960s and 1970s, and became less supportive of Israel. This last point is significant since a substantial

percentage of neoconservatives were Jewish intellectuals from the northeastern part of the country, prominent in academia, think tanks such as the American Enterprise Institute, and journals such as *Commentary*. Among the best known were Irving Kristol, Norman Podhoretz, Midge Decter, and Ben Wattenberg. There were, though, important non-Jewish individuals such as Jeane Kirkpatrick and William Bennett.

At first, there was a question as to whether neoconservatism would emerge as a permanent classification or whether it was merely a way station as these people migrated from liberalism into conservatism. Some continued to evolve, some remained as overall liberals who supported national security, but there has developed neoconservatism as a separate category. By the late 1980s, Kirk recognized this. Earlier, his anticommunism, his being a "Cold Warrior," had him supporting the Reagan coalition. But, as the Reagan presidency wound down, it was becoming clearer that the conservative consensus was evaporating, that differences were appearing, and that separate agendas were more evident. Especially troubling was a secular tinge, acceptance of too much big government, and too much Wilsonian interventionism—the idea that we Americans could and should intervene around the world not to protect ourselves and our friends, something Kirk advocated, but to spread "democratic capitalism." These Wilsonian types believed that once people around the world were exposed to these ideas they eagerly would embrace them. This Kirk considered shallow and utopian. Change does come, but it is not as quick or as simple as the neoconservatives believe; cultures and people are complex. After all, it took generations of gradual development in the West for order, justice, and freedom to sink their roots and for institutions defending them to become effective. Even here, they continually must be renewed. Other cultures cannot be expected simply to adopt our forms of government and have them at once take root and flourish; change takes time.

He wrote in *The American Cause* that "The American mission is not to make all the world one America, but rather to maintain America as a fortress of principle and in some respects an example to other nations." (TAC, 19) He believed that neoconservative misconceptions led this country into a major blunder in Vietnam, "the notion that we could establish or prop up in Viet Nam a 'democracy' that never had existed anywhere in southeastern Asia." (POP, 184)

A recent example of neoconservative naiveté was the expectation that the 2003 freeing of Iraq from Saddam Hussein would be akin to the freeing of Western Europe from Nazi oppression following D. Day—June 6, 1944. These Europeans took control of their countries once the Nazis were driven out and restored order, justice, and freedom, principles which had been well established there for generations. No doubt the neoconservatives who ran Bush Administration foreign policy sincerely believed that freeing Iraq would duplicate what had happened in Europe. Iraq still may develop standards of order, justice, and freedom such as we have. It may not, but if it does, it will have been far more difficult and taken far longer than the neoconservatives believed.

But, back to Kirk and the late 1980s and the early 1990s. He opposed the drift back to bigger government under George H. W. Bush and, especially, opposed the Persian Gulf conflict of 1990–1991, stating in his memoir that

"...during 1991 Kirk would come to detest Bush for his carpet-bombing of the Cradle of Civilization with its taking of a quarter of a million lives in Iraq." (TSI, 465) Kirk was concerned that the United States was moving to impose our culture on others, something he not only believed wrong, but also something which, based on his study of history, was doomed to fail. Earlier, he had stated in *The American Cause* that "America is the least imperialistic, probably, of all the great powers in all history." (TAC, 136) This, he feared, could be changing. In an address given to the Heritage Foundation, Kirk set forth his belief concerning what the nature of American leadership in the world should be:

> If we are to experience a Pax Americana, it will not be the sort of American hegemony that was attempted by Presidents Truman and Eisenhower and Kennedy and Johnson: not a patronizing endeavor, through gifts of money and of arms, to cajole or intimidate all the nations of the earth into submitting themselves to a vast over-whelming Americanization, wiping out other cultures and political patterns.
>
> An enduring Pax Americana would be produced not by bribing and boasting, but by quiet strength—and especially by setting an example of ordered freedom that might be emulated. (RTT, 179)

Foreign Policy

This consideration of neoconservatism is a natural transition into an examination of Kirk's beliefs about American foreign policy. This was not a major focus of his thought, but clear convictions stand out in his writings, fiction as well as nonfiction. The Kirk of the late 1930s and early 1940s was typical of much of the United States, especially the Midwest, during that time. He certainly opposed the imperialism of Japan, Germany, and Italy, but opposed intervention by this country. After Pearl Harbor, there was no question of his supporting the war effort. His dream of being a pilot in the air force (then the army air corps) collapsed because his eyes were not good enough. Then, as was discussed in the section on his life, he was drafted and served in the army until 1946. He did his duty well, but was most unenthusiastic about the armed forces for a period of time while also evincing a rather libertarian aversion to overseas escapades. The reality of the Soviet threat to justice and freedom shook him from this into a supporter of Barry Goldwater, Richard Nixon, and Ronald Reagan.

Yet it is intriguing to note that among the professions dreamed of by the young Kirk was that of soldier (TSI, 1). Also, the hero of his novel, *A Creature of the Twilight*, was Manfred Arcane, a soldier who had seen much combat, and a significant amount of the book was devoted to Arcane's successful leading of the legitimate government forces of a fictitious country in the northwestern quarter of Africa against a Soviet Union-backed revolt. Since Manfred Arcane dominated two of Kirk's three novels and two of his short stories, he does give insight into his originator. Much they had in common, perhaps of other things Kirk had dreamed.

Arcane was born in Vienna before World War I, the illegitimate son of an English nobleman and a Gypsy dancer. Although raised by his mother, he was educated thanks to his father's money, a substantial portion of which he inherited following that gentleman's death in World War I.

Seeking his own role in this world, Arcane became a soldier of fortune. In the novel, he said, referring to himself: "Thus must he be content with boots, saddles, spurs, and bright arms. Not wholly relishing, at all times, the company of a brutish and licentious soldiery, desultorily he read in the historians and the romancers." (COTT, 239) Arcane fought in colonial conflicts for both the British and the French, served with the Spanish Nationalist forces during the Spanish Civil War, and had many adventures during World War II in covert operations against the Nazis. Now, at the time the novel was set, he was minister without portfolio, the real power behind the throne, and the commander of the armed forces which preserved the freedom of the mythical country of Hamnegri, thereby thwarting an attempt by the Soviets to expand their empire into this part of Africa. In this book, Kirk also used the sharp edge of his humor to skewer naïve left wing diplomats and journalists who spouted pious platitudes while failing to find any serious threat to freedom and justice from the Soviet side of the Iron Curtain. He definitely believed that there were times when military force must be used to defend order, justice, and freedom.

Although asserting that Kirk sought to live through Manfred Arcane would be rather presumptuous, there are a number of intriguing similarities. Arcane was a Roman Catholic of middle years, well-read, given to flowery speech, and, by the end of the book, married to a strikingly beautiful younger woman. Certainly Kirk's anticommunism and support of tradition were reflected by Arcane. Perhaps too there was at some level within Kirk a soldier/adventurer who never manifested himself, except in fiction.

After the demise of the Soviet Union, Kirk again became more of a noninterventionist. Of course, during the early

1990s, the United States faced no security threat comparable to that posed by its old adversary. His previously discussed opposition to the imposition of Americanism was part of his disillusionment with George H. W. Bush's administration and led to his support of Pat Buchanan's challenge to the president in the 1992 primary season. In addition, Kirk and Buchanan had in common Roman Catholicism and a conservative philosophy which ran deeper than just disagreement with Bush foreign policy.

Multiculturalism

Kirk rejected the fad of multiculturalism as a force of civilizational destruction. It is one thing to be multiethnic; it is entirely different to be multicultural. To proclaim that the United States is a multicultural country, that the basis of our culture is diversity, is a statement empty of meaning. That would mean that there is no national culture, that this country is just a conglomeration of separate, unassimilated groups of people. To be successful, though, a country must be based on voluntarily accepted principles which unite people from diverse backgrounds. There must be something which transcends the differences which separate us. Robert Bork recognized this danger and wrote of it in *Slouching Toward Gomorrah: Modern Liberalism and American Decline*. He stated that had this country been as culturally divided at the time of our founding as it is today, we would not have won our independence and successfully founded a new country. Bork is correct concerning the forces of disunity gnawing away at our foundation. Actually, there was a significant amount of disunity here in the late eighteenth century, but, in the providence of God, leaders of great ability, courage, learning, and imagination overcame the problems and won. The same can be done today if, God willing, we once again raise up and support leaders with these qualities. Bork saw the barbarians at the gate; the situation indeed is perilous, but he was hopeful that reawakening and renewal will sweep through our land.

As Kirk stated it in *America's British Culture*, "A nation's traditional culture can endure only if the several elements that compose it admit an underlying unity or fidelity to a common cause." (ABC, 6) The American people come from varied ethnic backgrounds and are diverse in terms of professional and personal interests; tastes vary widely concerning music, literature, and sports. Yet, historically, we all have been American's supporting the same British-derived political and legal system, believing in a common set of civic virtues—church and family, duty, honor, and work.

Kirk set forth four ways in which our American culture was shaped by our British heritage:

> The first of these three ways is the English language and the wealth of great literature in that language. Bestriding the world, that English language should be of even greater advantage to Americans today than it has been in the past.
>
> The second of these ways is the rule of law, American common law and positive law being derived chiefly from English law. This body of laws gives fuller protection to the individual person than does the legal system of any other country.
>
> The third of these ways is representative government, patterned upon British institutions that began to develop in medieval times, and patterned especially upon "the mother of parliaments," at Westminster.

The fourth of these ways is a body of *mores*, or moral habits and beliefs and conventions and customs, joined to certain intellectual disciplines. These compose an ethical heritage. According to Tocqueville, Americans' *mores* have been the cause of the success of the American Republic. (ABC, 11)

Kirk was emphatic that these mores, indeed our whole culture, spring forth from Christian roots (ABC, 70–73). A body of such principles must be the foundation of a successful civilization which protects order, justice, and freedom. Otherwise, since chaos cannot exist for long, the alternative is arbitrary government without justice and freedom which would be imposed either by the dictatorship of one individual or a few people or a despotism by the majority. The eighteenth-century French philosopher Jean Jacques Rousseau proclaimed the doctrine of the general will, the belief that the standards and dictates of the majority are supreme, not subject to any other authority. In *The Social Contract*, he wrote that:

As nature gives each man absolute power over all his members, the social compact gives to the body politic absolute power over all its members also; and it is this power which, under the direction of the general will, bears, as I have said, the name of Sovereignty (Rousseau, 1952: 396–397).

Rousseau had no fears that democratic despotism would arise. Of this sovereignty, he stated:

Again, the Sovereign, being formed wholly of the individuals who compose it, neither has nor can have any interest contrary to theirs; and consequently the sovereign power need give not guarantee to its subjects, because it is impossible for the body to hurt all its members (Rousseau, 1952: 392). The majority, then, is subject to no restraints. The Commandments of God, written constitutions, and hallowed traditions, all would fall and be trampled before the onslaught of the sovereign majority. Sir Henry Sumner Maine, the nineteenth-century English scholar, wrote of Rousseau's espousal of the "omnipotent democratic State," warning his readers that it:

... has at its absolute disposal everything which individual men value, their property, their persons, and their independence; the State which is bound to respect neither precedent nor prescription.... (Maine, 1976: 165)

The Commandments of God are not subject to democratic approval in order for them to be valid and enforceable. There is no human legislative body with the authority to debate divine law, approving what it likes and rejecting what displeases it.

Today, the majority of Americans come from non English-speaking backgrounds; they preserve their pride of heritage, hold ethnic festivals, and pass on to succeeding generations an appreciation for their origins. Yet all have become Americans, integrated into a common culture rooted in voluntarily shared values. The "melting pot" has worked and is a key factor in our greatness.

Certainly Kirk understood that no culture endures forever, that history is filled with not just rises, but also falls. Still, he by no means despaired for our future. There is no inevitability to our decline; we have the capacity to reject the multiculturalist ideology with its shallow ethnic vanities and its desire to tear down our Anglo-American culture and we can renew what has been done well for so long. To give Russell Kirk the last word on the matter, he concluded the main part of *America's British Culture* with this encouragement:

> "Culture, with us ends in headache," Ralph Waldo Emerson wrote of Americans in 1841. Should the multi-culturalists have their way, culture, with us Americans a century and a half later, would end in heartache—and in anarchy. But to this challenge of multiculturalism, presumably the established American culture, with its British roots, still can respond with vigor—a life-renewing response. Love of an inherited culture has the power to cast the envy and hatred of that culture's adversaries. (ABC, 92)

Kirk's Christianity

In 2006, Dermot Quinn of Seton Hall University wrote for the *Political Science Reviewer* a laudatory, often perceptive essay on Russell Kirk entitled "Religion and *The Conservative Mind*" which, however, was wide of the mark in some of the conclusions presented. First of all, Quinn looked too much into *The Conservative Mind* for an understanding of Kirk's religious beliefs. Although regarded as Kirk's magnum opus, this book was published in 1953 before his faith really had developed, let alone matured. The principal ingredients of his philosophy were clear by then, but the foundation on which they would come to rest was still in the process of being formed. One who wishes to understand Kirk's beliefs is better advised to seek them in books such as *The Sword of Imagination, Redeeming the Time, The Roots of American Order,* and *The Conservative Constitution.* Quinn made a number of misleading statements which relegated Kirk's Christianity in general, his Roman Catholicism in particular, to a place of secondary significance. For example, he alleged that "Strongly anti-utilitarian, Kirk seems to share the utilitarianism he reprobated in others, reducing religion to sacred glue holding together the secular order." (Quinn, 2006: 8) Along the same line, Quinn further commented that "'In the church I see not the mystery of the incarnation,' Napoleon once said, 'but the mystery of the social order.' Kirk sometimes comes uncomfortably close to the same idea."

These assertions, though, are in error. Certainly Kirk saw Christianity as the foundation of civilization, but his faith went deeper than mere Benthamite utilitarianism. In *Redeeming the Time,* he stated that:

> For Jeremy Bentham notwithstanding, the Church is not a moral police force. What the Church always has been meant to do, really, is to offer a pattern for ordering the soul of the believer; and to open a window upon the transcendent realm of being. It is true that mastery of the theological virtues ought to follow upon sincere belief, and that sometimes it does so follow. Certainly there would be little virtue in our civilization, and quite possibly there would exist no modern civilization at all, were it not for Christian preaching of the theological virtues. (RTT, 62)

He further stated that:

> Knowing that this earthly existence is not the be-all and end-all, the church holds that perfect justice is in the

power of God alone, beyond the confines of time and space. In this world here below, we mete out justice as best we may. Sometimes we err in our administration of justice, it cannot well be otherwise; we are not perfect or perfectible creatures. (RTT, 192)

These are far from being the words of a Benthamite. In the June 2003 issue of *Touchstone*, Eric Scheske concluded that Kirk was a Christian, saying of him that:

His life was marked by Christian virtue: a good father and husband, a charitable man who cared for the poor and downtrodden, a writer who labored in God's vineyard in an age that tramples his grapes....A few more such Christians and contemporary civilization might be redeemed by now. (Scheske, 2003: 48)

Yet, two pages prior to this accolade, Scheske took a different tack when discussing the interaction of Kirk's early Stoicism and his later Christianity. He alleged that "Kirk never seemed to get over his Stoicism completely, so much so that his wife would refer to him years later as a Stoic rather than a Christian." (Scheske, 2003: 46) To warrant that assertion, he cited *The Sword of Imagination*, p. 231. There, though, the reader encounters something rather different: "Forty years later, Kirk's wife, bred up in high orthodoxy, would call her husband a Stoic still. Quite as there subsists a Christian humanism, there endures Christian Stoicism." (TSI, 231) Annette Kirk never averred that Russell was a Stoic rather than a Christian. As he himself stated, his Christianity underlay his whole being; his Stoicism was more a personality trait than anything deeper. Certainly he was no disciple of Xeno. His temperamental tendency in this direction was countered by an optimism rooted in faith.

"O Death, where is thy sting? O Grave, where is thy victory?" That promise it was which caused Christian faith to rise upon the ashes of the classical culture; that promise, renewed and believed afresh, may yet breathe vitality into a dissolving moral order. (TSI, 342)

Jeffrey Hart also disparages Kirk's faith when in his generally commendable history of *National Review, The Making of the American Conservative Mind,* he stated that "Luther had said, 'a mighty fortress is our God.' Kirk might say, 'A mighty fortress is my library.'" The juxtaposition of these statements is demeaning to Kirk's Christian belief. Hart, attempting to sire a bon mot, was too clever by a half, a trap into which academics are prone to fall.

Kirk's faith in fundamental Christian doctrine was evident and was set forth in numerous places. Letting him speak for himself is the best way to gain insight into his innermost being. He wrote in *The Roots of American Order* that:

The individual man being too weak to choose the way of Christ, God must choose him. Those whom God redeems are the "elect," brands snatched from the fires of lust for reasons only God knows. Out of His compassion, God saves some, by His grace leading their steps aright.

We cannot guess who these elect are. Worldly success is no sign of man's having been chosen by God, and those who think themselves righteous may be self-deceived. It is not good works that will save a man (though if a man loves God, charity and justice should flow from his faith): only divine intervention redeems him. Yet seek the city of God, through faith and prayer; repent; follow in Christ's steps. Then perhaps to you, all unworthy, grace may be given. (RAO, 162–163)

Most of this is solidly Christian with Augustinian/Calvinist overtones. The last two sentences, though, reflected the thought of, among others, some of the New England Puritans that perhaps we could prepare ourselves to be chosen by God, something contrary to the beliefs of Augustine, Thomas Aquinas, and Calvin.

Kirk's faith was secure, but he was fascinated by evidences of the senses which could reinforce it. The Shroud of Turin was a graphic example. He believed it to be the burial shroud of Christ, bearing His image, left there as something akin to a photographic positive. Kirk suggested that, if the Shroud were verified, it could prove to be a theophanic event or the forerunner to one which would have dramatic consequences, even leading to a return to an Age of Faith (TSI, 245–246).

W. Wesley McDonald, in *Russell Kirk and the Age of Ideology*, wrote that "It is possible, in my judgment, to present Kirk's contributions as a conservative thinker without having to consider their hypothetical Catholic aspect." (McDonald, 2004, 11–12) While that can be done, it is inadequate and gives a very incomplete view of the middle and later stages of Kirk's career. It is akin to analyzing Karl Marx's economics without considering his atheistic economic determinism.

Although Kirk did not perceive his calling to be that of an apologist for Roman Catholicism, his adherence to that system was sincere. Much of what he affirmed, such as the Apostles' Creed, was generic Christianity. To that he added distinctives such as papal infallibility and purgatory. Kirk came to Roman Catholicism as the culmination of years of thought and study, leading to the conclusion that civilizations and individuals without a theological foundation cannot survive and that Christianity is true. His search and growth led him to Rome because of its universality, antiquity, and, at least into the 1950s and early 1960s, traditionalism in practice. He accepted fully. His love for Annette, a devout Roman Catholic, had the effect of focusing his mind more intently and accelerating the pace of his entrance into the Church, but undoubtedly he would have ended there anyway, albeit somewhat later.

In a number of his fictional tales, short stories such as "Lex Talionis," "Saviourgate," and "Watchers at the Strait Gate,"[9] he set forth his belief in purgatory as a cleansing preparation whereby the just are prepared for entrance into, as stated in Matthew 25:21, "the joy of the Lord."

Still, though, Kirk was no narrow sectarian. He admired the Calvinist Jonathan Edwards, writing of him in *The Roots of American Order* that "Directly or indirectly, most Americans were moved by Edwards' powerful intellectual defense of revealed religion." (RAO, 340) Furthermore, he defended Shelton College against attacks by the state of New Jersey. The institution, no longer in existence, had been founded by Carl McIntire, a fiery clergyman who had been associated with J. Gresham Machen in opposing the growing theological and political liberalism in the Presbyterian Church in the late 1920s into the 1930s. McIntire subsequently became the key leader in establishing the Bible Presbyterian Church, the American Council of Christian Churches, and the International Council of Christian Churches. In addition to Shelton College, he also was instrumental in the opening of Faith

Theological Seminary in Pennsylvania and Highland College in California. Among his stances was a vehement rejection of Roman Catholicism. Kirk rose above that and, recognizing the principle of educational freedom, especially for Christian institutions, worked for the independence of Shelton College against the depredations of the state.

Although Kirk was not a systematic theologian nor a Catholic apologist, he did believe Christian verities were the foundation of Western Civilization, but he did not stop there; to that was added a deep personal Christian faith, something insufficiently recognized by many who have sought to understand him. The record is there to be discovered by those who probe, especially his works after the 1960s. His philosophy did not change after *The Conservative Mind* of 1953, but his Christian underpinning grew progressively stronger.

Church and State

When someone believes deeply in principles dealing with right and wrong, truth and error, it then becomes necessary to determine how to relate this belief to government. What should be enforced? What should be left to individual choice? Answers have ranged from totalitarian systems to devotees of anarchy with many lines being drawn between these extremes. For Christians, this is a matter of critical concern. In Western Civilization, relations between church and state have run the gamut from church domination of the state to state domination of the church.

The first position reached its zenith in 1302 when Pope Boniface VIII proclaimed in Unum Sanctum that:

Wherefore both are in the power of the church, namely, the spiritual and the material swords; the one, indeed to be wielded by the Church, the other for the Church; the former by the priest, the latter by the hand of kings and knights, but at the will and sufferance of the priest. For it is necessary that one sword should be under another and that the temporal authority should be subjected to the spiritual. (Ehler, 1957: p. 36)

On a few occasions, this papal assertion of power worked, as when Gregory VII brought to heel, albeit temporarily, the Holy Roman Emperor Henry IV and when King John of England swore allegiance to Innocent III as his feudal overlord. Most of the time, though, powerful monarchs, while giving lip service to papal claims of political suzerainty, did as they wished.

The polar opposite of this is caesaropapism, state control of the church. This can be seen in the Eastern Romans (Byzantine) Empire. For example, Emperor Justinian I (527–565) believed that the church and the state both were created by God, that each must respect the other, but that the state is the stronger of the two. In the West, Charlemagne, emperor from 800 to 814, believed much the same. He saw himself as the vicar of God, his empire as a reflection of the heavenly kingdom, and the authority of the pope as limited to spiritual matters. Caesaropapism also flourished under the Russian Czars beginning with Peter the Great (1682–1725). In effect, the church was a department of the state. Perhaps the high point of this doctrine occurred when the English Parliament passed the Act of Supremacy in 1534 during the reign of Henry VIII:

Be it enacted by authority of this present Parliament that the King our Sovereign Lord, his heirs and

successors kings of this realm, shall be taken, accepted,
and reputed the only Supreme Head in earth of the
Church of England called Anglicana Ecclesia, and shall
have and enjoy annexed and united to the Imperial
Crown of this realm as well that title and style thereof,
as all honours, dignities, preeminences, jurisdiction,
privilege, authorities, immunities, profits, and com-
modities, to the said dignity of Supreme Head of the
same Church belonging and appertaining. (Hughes
and Fries, eds. 1939: 47)

It should be noted that the position of Supreme Head
was legal in intent and effect. At no time did Henry and
his successors function as clergy. Today, the title has little
power attached to it.

John Calvin adopted a balanced view, teaching that
church and state are institutionally and functionally separate, that one does not dominate the other. Each was created by God and each is subject to Him.

Kirk did not fall into either of the extreme positions nor
was he a secularist who wanted religious influence out of
our civilization or, at most, in a corner within private lives
where it holds its peace and does not influence anything
beyond the individual. He was a Christian who believed
in religious freedom. He was firm in his assertion that the
Founders believed that Christianity was "intended to govern the soul, not to govern the state." (TCC, 130) In the
next sentence, however, he was equally firm that a good
society must be based on religious convictions. He was
well aware of the problems for justice and freedom that
have resulted from the mingling of religion and government, but considered the alternative worse: "There exists
something worse even than the confounding of religion

and politics: I mean total separation of religion from the civil social order." (TCC, 131)

Nothing in the U.S. Constitution mandates anything such as that. In only two places in it is religion mentioned. Article VI ordered that "no religious test shall ever be required as a qualification to any office or public trust under the United States" and the First Amendment which, among other things, stipulated that "Congress shall make no law respecting an establishment of religion, or prohibiting the free exercise thereof." The ongoing church-state controversies revolve around what is meant by "an establishment of religion: and what is meant by "the free exercise thereof."

Concerning the First Amendment, especially the prohibiting of "an establishment of religion," Kirk quoted Joseph Story who served on the United States Supreme Court from 1811 until 1845. Widely regarded as our preeminent constitutional scholar, Story wrote in his *Commentaries on the Constitution* that:

> Probably at the time of the adoption of the Constitution and of the First Amendment ... the general if not the universal sentiment in America was that Christianity ought to receive encouragement from the state so far as was not incompatible with the private rights of conscience and the freedom of religious worship. An attempt to level all religions, and to make it a matter of state policy to hold all in utter indifference, would have created universal disapprobation, if not universal indignation. (TCC, 132)

This expressed well what was believed by both Story and Kirk, that religion in this country should not be seen as merely a private matter but rather be recognized as the foundation of our culture, including government. Kirk stopped short of calling for a formal Christian common-wealth. It was his conviction that Christianity does influence the political order, indeed should do so, but that "there is a gulf fixed between influence of this sort, and presumptuous issuing of political prescripts to legitimate political authorities." (TCC, 140) So then, how should Christianity interact with and influence the state? Kirk set forth three ways: (1) its influence upon political leaders; (2) its influence upon the mass of people; and (3) its influence upon the shaping of societal norms.

Again citing Story, Kirk agreed that even though the United States has no constitutionally mandated establishment of religion, the laws and the civil institutions of this country are grounded in the teachings and, therefore, approved this de facto establishment which was in place into the second half of the twentieth century. During recent decades, there have been more assaults on this position from those who wish to expunge Christian influence from our civil order, in effect replacing it with a secular humanist establishment. Examples of this are U.S. Supreme Court rulings striking down organized prayer and devotional Bible reading in public schools along with prohibiting the display of the Ten Commandments there. The list of our attempts to de-Christianize our public life goes on and on. Opposition to this has strengthened, however, as increasing numbers of people have awakened to this menace and have mounted impressive renewals of our traditional beliefs. The culture conflict is intense.

In one of his lectures for the Heritage Foundation, Kirk summed up the civilizational contribution of Christianity:

Yet out of the ruins of Rome grew the highest order of liberty man has known: Christian freedom. The depressed masses of the proletariat were given hope by the promise of Christ; the barbarians were taught restraint by the Word. Humanity learnt the lesson of the suffering servant, and came to know that the service of God is perfect freedom. (RTT, 31)

As can be observed from reading the above, Kirk was no secular humanist nor was he a devotee of either Boniface VIII or of Peter the Great. Christianity must underlie our civilization if we are to enjoy the blessings of order, justice, and freedom, but the church is not to dictate to the government. Kirk did believe that the government should be active in certain cultural matters; he supported the pro life position that unborn human beings deserve legal protection against having their lives taken simply because they are unwanted and he considered pornography to be a socially destructive influence rather than a freedom-of-expression matter. His ideal was a government which reflected the voluntarily Christian society which elected it. Falling short of that ideal, something Kirk understood to be more likely than not, we strive to establish reasonable facsimiles of the ideal and constantly push on to do better.

Natural Law

In addition to divine revelation, Kirk also looked, albeit secondarily, to natural law. Some thinkers maintain that natural law originated with human beings or with nature, but Kirk and other Christians are adamant that natural law comes from God and can be ascertained apart from revelation.

In his biography of Kirk, Gerald J. Russello alleged that, although Kirk did believe in some form of natural law, "he was never clear about its sources and never discussed its precepts in any detail." (Russello, 2007: 8) In the same vein, W. Wesley McDonald in his biography of Kirk, claimed that concerning natural law principles Kirk "never explicitly defined them nor explained how man apprehends the dictates of natural law." (McDonald, 2004: 71) He further charged that Kirk "made no distinction between the moral imagination and natural law." (McDonald, 2004: 74) Also, "It is apparent that the blurring of distinctions between reason and imagination did not deeply trouble him." (McDonald, 2004: 74 n) Finally, he made reference to "Kirk's inchoate moral epistemology." (McDonald, 2004: 78)

This last opinion of Kirk is the easiest to comment upon. "Inchoate" means "disorderly" and "chaotic." One may wish, perhaps, that Kirk had been more systematic at times, more explicit, but he was not disorderly or chaotic in his thinking or in his writing. For the rest, since Kirk set forth general principles and did not seek to produce a rigid orthodoxy, to some extent people can see what they want to see or fear to see. But, Kirk did make clear statements on natural law. The best course is to let him speak for himself. The following three short quotations from *The Conservative Mind*, *The Roots of American Order*, and *Redeeming the Time* address points raised by Russello and McDonald.

Real harmony with the natural law is attained through adapting society to the model which eternal nature, physical and spiritual, sets before us....We are part of an eternal natural order which holds all things in their places. (TCM, 64)

Properly understood, the law of nature is the moral imagination,[10] and that natural law enables us, through reason, to apply customary and statutory law humanely. (RAO, 112)
Permit me to repeat here that the natural law is more than a guide for statesmen and jurists. It is meant primarily for the governance of persons—for you and me, that we may restrain will and appetite in our ordinary walks of life. Natural law is not a harsh code that we thrust upon other people: rather, it is an ethical knowledge, innate perhaps, but made more clearly known to us through the operation of right reason. And the more imagination with which a person is endowed, the more will he apprehend the essence of the natural law, and understand its necessity. (RTT, 200)

To hearken back to the contentions of Russello and McDonald, when Kirk's writings on Christianity and natural law are taken as a whole, there is no question that he did believe in God as the beginning point of everything, including natural law. Natural law, therefore, comes from God; identified with the moral imagination, it is innate and is aided in its operation by reason. On the role of reason, he stated that "In the Christian world the natural law was received as a body of unwritten rules depending upon universal conscience and common sense, ascertainable by right reason." (RTT, 198) Kirk explained further that natural law cannot replace legislatures and courts. He referred to his experience as a justice of the peace, an office which no longer exists under the present Michigan Constitution, for Morton Township of which Mecosta is part. When charged with determining which of two farmers was right in a boundary dispute, he did not use natural law theories to ascertain which claimant was more worthy, but rather used statutes, common law, local custom, and filed deeds. Natural law provides general principles, not precise answers to all questions (RTT, 204–205).

In order to illustrate the operation of natural law in human society and to give examples of general principles, Kirk drew upon C. S. Lewis's *The Abolition of Man* in which Lewis set forth eight natural laws found in religions and civilizations around the world. Two examples are honoring parents and providing properly for children. Yes, these are taught in the Bible, God's revelation, but they also are innate and can be reached by reason (RTT, 199).

Natural law has been misused by those who chafe at constitutional restrictions. As a significant example of that misuse, Kirk discussed the majority ruling in *Roe v. Wade* that there is a "right to privacy" in the U.S. Constitution which individualizes the ultimate decision on whether or not to take the life of an unborn infant. This "right" is not explicitly stated in the Constitution, but rather something these justices "perceived." This Kirk labeled a private judgment, which was contrary to natural law. As a Roman Catholic, he believed that the church is the authoritative interpreter of natural law (RTT, 211). To those outside of Roman Catholicism who believe that God is the source of natural law, this ruling is contrary to the natural law principle of loving care for children. Law superior to human law does exist, but appeals to it above constitutions and statutes must be done with care so that God is being obeyed rather than personal beliefs being exalted.

Democracy, Aristocracy, and the American Founding

Kirk wrote in *The Conservative Constitution* that at least 50 of the 55 men who met in Philadelphia during the summer of 1787 would have subscribed to the Apostles' Creed, although the gentlemen's code then prevailing frowned on religious outspokenness[11] (TCC, 43). These men, being fundamentally Christian in terms of their beliefs about human nature, unlike those who led the French Revolution 2 years later, did not seek to create a perfect society but rather aimed at devising a practical formula for the best possible government. Kirk did not consider the Deism of some men such as Thomas Jefferson and Benjamin Franklin reflective of the beliefs of most Founders. Perfection is not of this world and attempts to create it lead to despair, chaos, and then dictatorship.

These men understood also the contributions of Athens and Rome to Western Civilization. They were well-read in the classics, having studied Cicero, Plutarch, and Vergil as well as English political history and English literature. This wealth of wisdom and learning was enriched by common sense and practical experience in the affairs of this world. They were men of talent and achievement, but they did not seek to solidify their positions to the detriment of others. They desired to see others rise,[12] they did not seek to level downwards and enforce equality as did the Levellers and the Diggers in seventeenth-century England and as would Marxists and many liberals from the nineteenth century to today.

When Kirk referred to them as gentlemen, he did not mean just those born into upscale families, "to the manor born," but to be a gentleman "signified outwardly manners and dress and speech; inwardly, a sense of honor and duty." (TCC, 45) But, Kirk favored a system in which people of routine abilities, interests, and motivation could be themselves, free from domination by the capable, industrious, successful individuals who control aristocratic societies. On the other hand, the achievers would not be crushed by the mass in a democratic society. Both Kirk and most of the Founders believed that this balance would be guarded best by a natural aristocracy, that is, one based on personal characteristics such as moral character and ability rather than on birth. In this there was concurrence even from most of the Founders who had sprung forth from upper class families. Kirk summed up his convictions on the point in the third of his six canons of conservative thought:

> Conviction that civilized society requires orders and classes, as against the notion of a "classless society." With reason, conservatives often have been called "the party of order." If natural distinctions are effaced among men, oligarchs fill the vacuum. Ultimate equality in the judgment of God, and equality before courts of law, are recognized by conservatives; but equality of condition, they think, means equality in servitude and boredom. (TCM, 8–9)

In 1957, *The American Cause* was published by Regnery. Kirk wrote it to provide a short book (172 pages) for the purpose of countering the all too widespread weak understanding in this country about our foundational principles and the institutions built on them. He later elaborated substantially on these themes in *The Roots of American Order* which came out in 1974. In *The American*

Cause, he declared that the men who wrote the United States Constitution, understanding that goodness and wisdom cannot be taken for granted, determined to balance interest and branches of government, preventing as well as they could any concentration of power which would bring down justice and freedom. This he believed they did impressively well.

Still, no matter how impressive the document, human beings must implement it and make its functioning a reality. Kirk pointed out in *The Roots of American Order* that the Constitution would not have established order, justice, and freedom had not the leaders at the time of ratification been men of outstanding character, capability, and determination. In particular, he cited the contributions of George Washington as the first president, of the members of Congress during the first decade after ratification, and of John Marshall as chief justice of the U.S. Supreme Court (RAO, 418–419).

Contrary to the politically correct exaltation of democracy so much in vogue, Kirk presented a much less favorable view.[13] In an article he wrote for the November 1988 issue of *The World and I,* he supported democratic political forms as a means for establishing and maintaining a decent, reasonable society. Since he did not believe that a perfect society could be created by human beings, he rejected the naiveté of those who saw democracy as an end in itself, as an ideal. Those who advocate this, people such as Jean Jacques Rousseau and those who look to him for enlightenment, proclaim that the people are sovereign; God fits into this either not at all or in a secondary role endorsing the will of the people. A strongly believing Christian, Kirk affirmed that God is sovereign and that the will of the people operates only within that context.

It is significant to note, Kirk wrote in the same article, that our Founders did not use democracy in a favorable sense, instead equating it with mob rule. They determined to create a federal republic, balancing the interests of the different elements of society and preserving freedom for all. No segment should be able to restrict the rights of the others, whether it be one person, a small group of people, or the majority.

Kirk agreed with the warnings about democratic despotism presented so eloquently by Alexis de Tocqueville in *Democracy in America*. Impressed with and optimistic about the United States, Tocqueville nevertheless was concerned lest this country and others which had adopted democracy, come to exalt mediocrity while tearing down achievement and quality, that the mass would oppress the ambitious and the capable. He feared further that a powerful central government would more and more take care of people, seducing them into no longer caring about freedom. As Kirk expressed Tocqueville's strictures about these matters:

> What menaces democratic society in this age is not a simple collapse of order, nor yet usurpation by a single powerful individual, but a tyranny of mediocrity, a standardization of mind and spirit and condition enforced by the central government....He foresaw the coming of the "social welfare state," which agrees to provide all for its subjects, and in turn exacts rigid conformity. (TCM, 208)

It was not Kirk's belief that all was lost, but enough of what Tocqueville warned against had sprouted in this country to warrant concern and to take corrective measures.

The social order of this country was sustained by the moral order which in turn grew out of the prevailing Christianity which suffused the United States through most of the years of our history and still does to some extent (RAO, 448). Kirk was convinced that there must be a set of moral principles accepted as authoritative or justice cannot live. But, he charged, modern liberals and democrats reject this very concept of an authority above and beyond them. He went on to state that unless they are checked in their attacks on what he referred to as "habitual reverence and prescriptive morality," that justice will be destroyed not just for the enemies of these people, but for themselves as well (RAO, 463). Kirk further asserted that the will of the people should prevail in society, but only under God, a qualification ignored by many liberals and democrats.

The American system of opening the prospects for influence and significance to a progressively wider segment of the population worked because of Christianity. "The power of Christian teaching over private conscience made possible the American democratic society." (RAO, 94–95)

Summation

Kirk strove to revive and strengthen the body of fundamental principles which he believed formed the essence of Western Civilization. Briefly these he articulated in the six canons and the ten principles of conservative thought. Kirk's Christian faith developed and deepened considerably during the middle and later years of his career. As sources of understanding and knowledge, he affirmed revelation, natural law, and reason in that order

of reliability and certainty. By no means did he dispar-
age reason, but, as a Christian he did not exalt it to the
supreme position. Kirk believed that God created all and,
ultimately, controls all, yet created human beings with the
freedom to accept Him or to reject Him, to base our civilization and our individual lives on His teachings or to follow human-devised ideologies.

Kirk maintained, along with Ortega y Gasset, that the
United States could not survive for long if a catastrophe
were to hit Europe (ABC, 83). It certainly is true that our
culture—our religious system, our governmental and judicial principles, our literature—crossed the Atlantic from
Europe, especially from Britain. It is not, however, axiom-
atic that a catastrophe in Europe would doom us. Although
the great centers from which Western Civilization arose
are all areas across the waters to the east of this country—
Jerusalem, Athens, and Rome—if we do better refurbish-
ing the noble aspects of our heritage, if we keep the roots
of our culture well-watered, then we in the United States
can take the lead in reviving our common civilization.

But, there are things to be corrected first. If we persist
in walking away from our heritage for fear that some may
become ethnocentric or that some may be offended by our
beliefs since they come from other cultures, then we will
end up without roots as a people, with no commonality to
pass on to future generations. A country with no cohesion,
with no unifying principles, will fail; it will not be able to
stand before the onslaught of those with an antipathy for
our culture and who have the vigor and determination to
replace it with something else.

Inherited civilizational capital can be run through and
exhausted just as is true of financial capital. This Kirk saw
signs of here in the United States. A key example was the

weakening of Christian faith and a change of the direction in which many leaders were taking their churches:

> Many of the clergy tend markedly toward a sentimental and humanitarian application of religious teachings; they incline toward the radical alteration of society at the expense of the transcendent ends of religion and of any personal obedience to moral teachings. (ABC, 84)

As an outgrowth of this, Kirk saw too much ignorance of human nature. He wrote of a conversation he had with a university student with a high IQ who thought it logical that we simply train an elite of governmental leaders and, trusting in their moral qualities and expertise, let them run the country (ABC, 85). If people lack education in Christian truths and the record of human experience, they well can think this way. Christianity, however, teaches clearly what human nature is like apart from God and history records what has happened when concentrated, unchecked power is in the hands of government leaders with no commitment to Him; order, justice, and freedom all are eroded. The only hope for their revival is a return to Him.

Kirk believed in freedom for the moral imagination to develop and soar. Often he was clear and systematic, but on other occasions his love for the joys of creativity was greater and he opened the door for the possibility of varying interpretations. Here comes to mind the parable from India of blind men attempting to describe an elephant. One felt its leg and concluded it is like a pillar. He who felt the tail said it is like a rope. The third felt the trunk and was convinced it was like a tree branch. The one who felt the ear was convinced it was like a hand fan. The fifth felt the belly and averred that an elephant is like a wall. The last, feeling the tusks, stated that it is like a solid pipe. The point is that they all were correct, but only in part; none of them could grasp the whole. So it is with Kirk. Some see him as a quaint eccentric, out of place in the world of today. Several of the variant interpretations will be discussed in the section on his reception.

When Kirk's writings are taken as a whole, however, clarity appears and consistency emerges. He wanted to set forth broad principles within which there was room for diversity. He took strong positions, as can be seen from reading the six canons, the ten principles, or for that matter, any of his books or essays, but he recoiled from any allegation that he was attempting dictation and control of others.

When writing of Sir Walter Scott, Kirk commented that through his novels he "disseminated Burke's conservative vision to a public that never would have read political tracts." (POP, 68) A similar motivation sparked Kirk's entry into fiction. To a certain extent, his writing novels and short stories was for the purpose of earning money to support his family. Partially too, they provided a means of relaxing and having fun. But, returning to the quotation about Scott, Kirk understood well that he could reach a different audience through fiction than through nonfiction. In addition to being good entertainment, these works extolled traditional virtues such as courage, consideration for others plus recognition of and rejection of evil. His progressively deepening Christian faith, especially is evident in his writings during the 1970s and the 1980s, such as *Saviourgate, Watchers at the Strait Gate, There's a Long, Long Trail A-Winding,* and *Invasion of the Church of the Holy Ghost.* These, along with the other short stories, have been anthologized in *Ancestral Shadows: An Anthology of Ghostly Tales.*

Kirk was a patriotic American, but by no means a chauvinistic condemner of everyone else. He did believe that the United States and the United Kingdom had done the best of all countries in establishing and furthering order, justice, and freedom. He did not contend that therefore others are inherently inferior and should be subjected. He loved this country and did not become an expatriate as did T. S. Eliot, but he certainly was quite at home in the U.K. especially in Scotland.

He had a deep love for a preindustrial, agrarian time in history, but certainly adjusted to living in a totally different era. He did use all the modern means of transportation[14] and communication, but deplored the all-too-frequent deleterious impact of an industrial society on religion, family, and neighborhood. But, he was, though, no Luddite wanting to destroy industry in order to recapture the past. The principles in which he believed and which he promoted are "the permanent things" which can live in and renew our industrial, technical civilization.

The implementation of all that Kirk taught requires maturity and seriousness of purpose for us in Western Civilization. It is all too common for people either to go their own individual ways, gratifying themselves apart from consideration of deeper matters or to want everything spelled out and nailed down for them. Kirk was aware of these tendencies, but, although sometimes discouraged by events, never was controlled by despair; he knew that in God's good time truth and right would triumph.

Visually summing up Kirk's worldview is a sculpture by Hew Lorimer, with whom he became friendly while traveling through Scotland during vacations from St. Andrews University. Lorimer was reputed to be the best of the Scottish sculptors in the middle of the twentieth

century. For generations the Lorimers had been one of
the Catholic gentry families of the land. A prized possession of Kirk's was the original relief model of the three
large relief figures Lorimer had carved for the National
Library of Scotland in Edinburgh. The central of the three
human figures is Theology in front of whom is the sword
of faith. To the right of Theology is Law, wearing a wig
and holding a book. On the other side of Theology stands
History, holding a scroll and a quill pen. Here are the key
components of a vital, healthy civilization. The model still
is on the wall above the fireplace in the Kirk library.

As he concluded his memoir, *The Sword of Imagination*,
Kirk, knowing that he had only a few weeks left to live,
summed up the goals he had set for his life. Not always
does a person have the realization that life in this world
is almost at an end yet enough time remains for careful
scrutiny of the years past. He discussed three ends or goals
which he had sought:

> One had been to defend the Permanent Things....He
> had sought to conserve a patrimony of order, justice,
> and freedom; a tolerable moral order; and an inheri-
> tance of culture. Although rowing against a strong tide,
> in this aspiration he had succeeded somewhat, certainly
> beyond his early expectation, in reminding people that
> truth was not born yesterday.
>
> A second had been to lead a life of decent indepen-
> dence, living much as his ancestors had lived, on their
> land, in circumstances that would enable him to utter
> the truth and make his voice heard: a life uncluttered
> and unpolluted, not devoted to getting and spending. In
> this antique vocation of man of letters, he had achieved
> that aspiration at Piety Hill.

A third end had been to marry for love and to rear children who would come to know that the service of God is perfect freedom. In his middle years the splendid Annette had given herself to him and then given him four children, presently endowed with the unbought grace of life. Annette and he helped to sustain the institution of the family by creating a vigorous example. (TSI, 473–474)

This indeed was a life well-lived!

Notes

1. Personally, I believe the inspiring and unifying qualities of the six canons outweigh Kirk's concern lest conservatism degenerate into something rigidly enforced.

2. The Frenchman Alexis de Tocqueville is the exception, but he wrote of the United States.

3. Universalists and Unitarians did not merge until 1961.

4. Kirk used "ideology" in a pejorative sense, never, as is done commonly, as synonymous with philosophy or belief system. To him, an ideology is a false system originated by human beings in opposition to the permanent things.

5. In *The Conservative Mind*, there is only one reference to him.

6. *Academic Freedom: An Essay in Definition* was published in 1955, *The Intemperate Professor, and other Cultural Splenetics* in 1965, and the most significant, *Decadence and Renewal in the Higher Learning* which came out in 1978. Kirk commented, perhaps "grumped" would be a better word, that the third of these books did not receive close to the amount of attention devoted to Alan Bloom's later *The Closing of the American Mind* even though they both covered much the same

ground (TSI, 433). In general, Kirk was at peace within himself and with himself, not prone to envy or regret, but, being human, occasionally he let the reader glimpse a small side of him that did not reflect the affable Christian Stoic who was in control most of the time.

7. As Kirk stated in *The Wise Men Know What Wicked Things Are Written on the Sky*:

> If college and university do nothing better than act as pretentious trade-schools; if their chief service to the person and the republic is to act as employment agencies—why, such institutions will have dehumanized themselves. They will have ceased to give us young people with reason and imagination who leaven the lump of any civilization. (WMK, 84)

8. The reader also is referred to *The Politics of Prudence* and *Redeeming the Time*.

9. The best compilation of Kirk's short stories is *Ancestral Shadows: An Anthology of Ghostly Tales* which was published by Eerdmans in 2004.

10. Kirk distinguished it from the diabolical imagination and the idyllic (utopian) imagination.

11. The question of the Founders' religious faith is a rather thorny one. Some historians, such as John Eidsmoe and Clarence Carson, agree with Kirk. Others, such as Mark Noll and Harold O. J. Brown, disagree, believing that the Christianity of these men was weaker than that of those who wrote the colonial charters and incorporated clearly Christian foundational statements in them. Certainly there were firm believers among the Founders such as John Jay (who was not at the Constitutional Convention), Roger Sherman, Richard Bassett, and John Witherspoon. A Christian worldview, at least, prevailed with them (Pafford, 2003: 51–54).

12. There were some among the Founders who believed in slavery and white supremacy.

13. He rejected the philosophy of vox populi vox dei, that is, that the voice of the people is the voice of God.

14. He could drive a car, but preferred not to, labeling the automobile a "mechanical Jacobin," something responsible directly and indirectly for altering negatively the ties between people and their communities and for adverse physical changes such as the proliferation of highways and roads (TSI, 49).

4

Reception of His Writings

To open this section, William F. Buckley succinctly presented the impact of Russell Kirk in general and of *The Conservative Mind* in particular, writing in his 1970 book *Did You Ever See a Dream Walking?: American Conservative Thought in the Twentieth Century* that:

> Russell Kirk may well be the best known "professional" conservative in America, by which adjective is meant that he launched his extraordinary career by an act of conscious apostleship to a social and historical and philosophical order which is best described as "conservative." His first spectacular was *The Conservative Mind*, a book on the ideas of prominent English and Americans that was arresting in its grasp of intellectual history. (Buckley, 1970: 218–219)

In the 1994 Russell Kirk memorial issue of *The University Bookman*,[1] William A. Rusher addressed the significance of *The Conservative Mind*, writing that:

> In this enormously influential book he almost single-handedly rooted American conservatism in the rich loam of the ancient Judeo-Christian tradition, and thereby gave it the philosophical heft of a world-view. (Rusher, 1984, p. 16)

Kirk's first book, *Randolph of Roanoke: A Study in Conservative Thought,* was published first in 1951; later editions, only moderately revised, came out in 1964 and 1978. It was well received on a modest level, only to be substantially overshadowed by *The Conservative Mind,* published 2 years later. It was this second book which catapulted Kirk to the forefront as a scholar of international renown. The timing of the publication of the book by Regnery was providential in terms of its getting favorably reviewed. Kirk earlier had praised a book written by Gordon Keith Chalmers, president of Kenyon College. Now, Chalmers returned the favor many times over in the *New York Times Book Review,* May 17, 1953. He opened his review with a summary of *The Conservative Mind* sure to warm the cockles of any author's heart:

> The author of *The Conservative Mind* is as relentless as his enemies, Karl Marx and Harold Laski, considerably more temperate and scholarly, and in passages of this readable book, brilliant and even eloquent. (Witalec, 2002: 242)[2]

This high praise by a respected academic in a prestigious journal guaranteed that serious attention would be accorded Kirk and *The Conservative Mind.* Chalmers went on to comment that in recent years it had been the left which most of the time had set the tone for philosophical and political discussions. This now has been changed by the Kirk counteroffensive against the liberals.

Time devoted the entire book review section of the July 6, 1953 issue to *The Conservative Mind.* In *The Sword of Imagination,* Kirk reported that Max Ways, an editor of *Fortune, Time*'s sister magazine, had been assigned the review. Kirk, never one for braggadocio nor one for false humility, was pleased when he was informed that Ways and many readers of the review were drawn into conservatism and that the first printing of *The Conservative Mind* quickly sold out (TSI, 149).

In his review, Ways referred to conservatism as a vigorous and growing force, with however, problems:

> But as a conscious and proudly defended outlook on public affairs, as a philosophy of life and government, it was driven underground for a hundred years, laughed out of the schools, driven like an old hag in a gunnysack from the glittering and shifting fashion show of ideas. "The Stupid Party" was what John Stuart Mill called the conservatives a century ago. It stuck. (Ways, 1953: 88)

Ways then proceeded to credit Kirk with reversing that situation, providing a genealogy of great minds and their ideas as the foundation of a modern movement now respectable and to be taken seriously.

Writing 30 years after the publication of *The Conservative Mind*, William A. Rusher in *The Rise of the Right* recounted the profound impact Kirk's book had on him. He already was an anticommunist, a rejecter of liberal domestic programs, and not impressed favorably by the new administration of Dwight Eisenhower. He wanted, though, something to favor rather than just being against this and that. *The Conservative Mind* filled the void:

> Kirk introduced me to the traditionalist heritage of Burkean conservatism, which dovetailed neatly with my instinctive hostility to the scientific, programmatic bent of all forms of Marxist socialism, including communism. He also endowed me—no small gift—with a

new and deeper understanding of the word conservatism. (Rusher, 1984: 28–29)

This was an admiring, appreciative reaction replicated
many times during the mid-1950s as the number of those
impacted deeply by Kirk grew.

The six canons are the best known part of *The Conservative
Mind*, being known to those who have not mastered the volume in its entirety. As was discussed earlier, over the years
since 1953, Kirk did pull back somewhat from an emphasis
on the six canons and the ten principles lest they come to
be accepted as written in granite, defining in an exacting
manner for all time precisely what conservatism is. Some
of those who admire deeply his thought agree with him.
An example is Gerald J. Russello who is the author of *The
Postmodern Imagination of Russell Kirk*, overall a study very
favorable to the subject. Russello, however, discussed his
misgivings about the six canons in an article he wrote for
the Spring/Summer 2003 issue of *The Intercollegiate Review*.
In it, he stated that although they are the most quoted part
of *The Conservative Mind*, they were the weakest part of the
book since they rendered Kirk vulnerable to the accusation of those "who thought they exemplified a conservative abstraction at odds with the historical texture of the
remainder of Kirk's account." (Russello, 2007: 11)

A ringing endorsement of *The Conservative Mind* in
general and of the six canons in particular was delivered
by Brainerd Cheney in the winter 1954 issue of *Sewanee
Review*. He credited Kirk with providing philosophical
lodestars by which civilization can navigate successfully. In
The Conservative Mind, Cheney averred:

Kirk makes a monumental contribution toward clarify-
ing the position of the conservatives in modern society,

he presents them with a challenging cause, and he lists impressive social and political resources for them. (Witalec, 2002: 250)

The six canons of conservative thought Cheney described as "compass headings." (Witalec, 2002: 247)

Also supportive of the canons were Paul Gottfried and Thomas Fleming who coauthored *The Conservative Movement* in 1988. They set forth their conviction that "although Kirk later denied the dogmatic intent of his 'canons of conservative thought,' his rigorous formulation may have given many conservatives a coherent philosophy for the first time." (Gottfried and Fleming, 1988: 13) There are Kirk followers galore who would drop the tentative "may have given," substituting "did give." Kirk appeared to have underestimated the need of most conservatives for a summary formulation of the beliefs they hold in common and which draw them together. The canons provide a central base from which conservatives sally forth into diverse areas of thought and, thence, action.

Gottfried and Fleming also appreciated Kirk's determination to do battle for right and truth here and now and the upbeat attitude he developed as he grew in Christianity:

Unlike Weaver, Kirk and his followers had not given up on the present age. They sought to restore America and the Western world to what they thought were its first principles. (Gottfried and Fleming, 1988: 13)

Two books written from the vantage point of conservative political action rather than conservative thought also praised the contributions of Kirk to developing the solid philosophical foundation without which meaningful political success would not be possible. The authors were battle-scarred veterans of the political arena who had experienced both defeat and victory. Richard A. Viguerie wrote the first, *The New Right: We're Ready to Lead*, which was published in 1981. Of Kirk, Viguerie wrote: "In 1953, Russell Kirk wrote the classic book, *The Conservative Mind*, which provided a solid philosophical base for American conservatism." (Viguerie, 1981: 47)

The other book, *Why Reagan Won: The Conservative Movement 1964–1981*, was coauthored by F. Clifton White and William J. Gill and it too was published in 1981. The authors looked back to three young thinkers of the 1950s who were at the forefront in building the idea base from which conservative electoral success arose. Chronologically in terms of key books they wrote they were Richard Weaver, William F. Buckley, and Russell Kirk. Of *The Conservative Mind* they wrote:

A study of conservative thought since the late 18th Century, Kirk's book was also a sweeping indictment of liberalism in all its forms. Looking back to Edmund Burke as the founder and fountainhead of "the true school on conservative principle," Kirk argued persuasively that any just government had to be grounded on the "belief that a divine intent rules society as well as conscience, that "property and freedom are inseparably connected, that economic leveling is not economic progress," and, finally, that there must be a "recognition that change and reform are not identical." (White and Gill, 1981: 33–34)

Donald Atwell Zoll analyzed Kirk's writings in the fall 1972 issue of *The Political Science Reviewer*. He identified three areas in which Kirk has presented himself to the reading public. They are: as the historian of ideas; as an essayist and social critic; and as a writer dedicated to belles lettres. In the first category, Zoll placed *The Conservative Mind* and Kirk's biographies of Randolph, Taft, Burke, and Eliot. In the second were, for example, *Enemies of the Permanent Things, A Program for Conservatives, The American Cause, Confessions of a Bohemian Tory,* and *Beyond the Dreams of Avarice.* His novels and short stories comprised the third category (Witalec, 2002: 253).

Overall, Zoll very much respected the contributions of Kirk to the revival of conservatism in the second half of the twentieth century. He did raise, though, a couple of situations in which he did not believe that Kirk was at his best. The first is Zoll's opinion that Kirk was not as effective when he left the realm of ideas to write on politics and to involve himself in political activity. There is some truth in these conclusions, but, Kirk did not do either frequently and Zoll did not acknowledge a key point about Kirk's political involvement. Certainly, Kirk was not primarily a political commentator or a political activist, but he did believe that those who espouse order, justice, and freedom have an obligation to involve themselves in the political process. He taught that politics deals with what is possible, that it cannot deliver to perfect. Zoll lamented that "admirable as they might be, Messrs. Taft and Goldwater could not fit into the palladium with Burke, Disraeli, Newman or Chesterton." (Witalec, 2002: 256) Of course, Burke, Disraeli, Newman, and Chesterton were not perfect themselves and Kirk well understood the limitations of politics, probably better than Zoll thought he did.

The Conservative Mind has proven to be the most influential of Kirk's writings. He was not, though, akin to a Mascagni or a Leoncavallo, composers who wrote one great opera each, respectively *Cavalleria Rusticana* and *I*

Pagliacci, but whose careers never again approached that level. Even though Kirk's later books did not ascend as high as *The Conservative Mind* in the estimation of most others, a good number of them were well received, sold well, and are still in print.

Kirk himself regarded *Enemies of the Permanent Things* as his favorite and his best work, a conviction close to that of Zoll who considered this Kirk's most impressive work since *The Conservative Mind.* In reference to Kirk's preferring it over his other works, it is interesting to note how often writers and composers do not share with the general public opinions on what are their most significant creations. Arthur Sullivan, most famed for the light operas he composed with William Gilbert as librettist, did not regard them as his best work and broke his partnership for a far less successful move into the ranks of grand opera composers. Also, Arthur Conan Doyle, best known for his Sherlock Holmes books and short stories, grew weary of the character and killed him off in one of his stories, only to be compelled by public pressure to bring him back. Among Kirk's nonfiction books, *Enemies of the Permanent Things,* well-reviewed to be sure, never rose as high with conservative readers as did *The Conservative Mind* and *The Roots of American Order.* With the former, Kirk was pleased, with the latter less so, considering it too much of a textbook in nature. But, here again, high praise came from others. Ray Bradbury wrote to Sherwood Sugden, the publisher of *The Roots of American Order* commending Kirk's fair-minded, balanced scholarship:

> In these polarized and emotional times we need more thinkers of excellence on both sides in order to make

fair decisions concerning our future. Russell Kirk is just such an excellent thinker. I hope his *The Roots of American Order* is read by fair-minded people of both left and right everywhere in our country.[3]

Bradbury also very much admired Kirk's fiction, noteworthy coming from a novelist of Bradbury's renown.

Standing high in the estimation of several reviewers was *Eliot and His Age*. Kirk became well acquainted with Eliot and was influenced by him; in particular, he was a key factor in Kirk's migration to Christianity. George Scott-Moncrieff, also a good personal friend of Kirk's, wrote a glowing review of *Eliot and His Age* which was published in the fall 1972 issue of *Sewanee Review*. As a lad, Scott-Moncrieff had met Eliot for the first time, already having been drawn to his writings previously. He continued to admire him greatly. In actuality, this study by Scott-Moncrieff is more a commentary on Eliot than it is a review of Kirk's book. Yet in the last paragraph, he refocuses, praising Kirk for what he did:

Dr. Kirk puts us all in his debt for assembling in a book at once detailed and immensely readable the creed of a man whose thought becomes only more relevant as the years pass. Eliot's conservatism certainly extends today from the conservation of civilized culture to the conservation of the ecology that sustains our very life. (Witalec, 2002: 253)

A more guarded review of *Eliot and His Age* was written by W. W. Robson, published in *Partisan Review*, winter 1973. He has no doubt that Eliot's fame as a poet will live on, but is more dubious about the prospects for his prose and for his plays to retain the high esteem in which they once were held. His opinions of Kirk's biography also are a mixed bag:

> Mr. Russell Kirk's *Eliot and His Age* is unlikely to become the standard literary biography. But it is an interesting and readable survey of Eliot's career, by an American friend of his later years. Mr. Kirk's approach is more informed and personal than academic.... Mr. Kirk is himself an exponent of a form of American conservatism which has quite a lot in common with Eliot's own position; and I found particularly interesting his attempts to relate the poet's political and social ideas to early American sources. It is in this area that Mr. Kirk makes perhaps his most distinctive contribution to the study of Eliot. He also deals extensively, in chronological sequence, with the poems, but I found his explications and paraphrases long-winded and his bluff and breezy manner somewhat incongruous. His book is excessively lengthened by these analyses, and further diluted by a continuous daubed-on commentary on "the march of events" in the England of Eliot's lifetime, which is always rather superficial and sometimes prejudiced and inaccurate. (Witalec, 2002: 265)

As generally is true when perusing reviews, the reader learns as much about the reviewer as about the subject of the review. It would be interesting to know what Robson found to be "sometimes prejudiced and inaccurate." The accusation that Kirk was "sometimes prejudiced" is not too surprising since it is quite common for people to so label those who disagree with them. The other allegation, that Kirk sometimes is "inaccurate" is more disturbing. While it is true that someone can be inaccurate because of an innocent error, there also is the implication of either poor scholarship or of a failure to be truthful. Kirk does not deserve either tag as part of his legacy. One may disagree with Kirk's conclusions, but to ascribe either poor scholarship or untruthfulness to his commentary is beyond the pale. Perhaps Robson did not intend to be that harsh, although his reference a few words earlier in the quotation that Kirk's commentary on the England of Eliot's lifetime was "always rather superficial" would tend to render that a vain hope. Superficiality is a strange tag to try to pin on Kirk.

To return to Zoll, he, writing in 1972, gave his opinion that *Eliot and His Age* was in many ways Kirk's best work up to that point. He attributed this to his being very comfortable with the subject and at ease which led to careful scholarship and to penetrating analyses of Eliot's thought and of the milieu in which he wrote, on the last point a sharply different conclusion from that of Robson. A possibly insightful comment by Zoll was that:

> There is a feeling of refreshment in *Eliot and His Age*, as if Kirk was enjoying a liberation from past confinements, was permitted to emerge, unabashedly, as what he most eminently is: a man of letters. (Witalec, 2002: 259)

This well could be. There is the reality that Kirk navigated successfully in several different seas, writing in no single genre; his nonfiction and fiction works were extraordinarily diverse, ranging through history, biography, economics, political science, social commentary, and academic policy, although consistent themes ran through them all.

In *Modern Age*, winter 1998, John Attarian wrote "Russell Kirk's Political Economy." He discussed Kirk's economics, emphasizing that his beliefs in that realm, along with all his other beliefs, were rooted in Christianity. He presented Kirk's endorsement of "a pattern of private property, competition in price and quality, freedom of economic choice, and satisfactory productivity." Attarian then quoted Kirk's stating of himself that he was "one of capitalism's friends, though no worshiper of idols." (Witalec, 2002: 325) By this, Kirk was affirming that Christianity is the source of ultimate meaning and that to seek that anywhere else was, in effect, to worship an idol.

Also, in the same article, Attarian defended Kirk against the attacks by James Nuechterlein of *First Things*, and by Martin Morse Wooster of *The American Enterprise*, attacks which will be presented later.

Zoll suggested that there are four characteristics of Kirk's thought that critics are likely to find irritating. He believed they would be bothered by Kirk's not being philosophically precise, his predominantly literary orientation, his firm theism, and his romanticism rooted in a bygone era (Witalec, 2002: 259, 260). Zoll initiated his defense of Kirk on the first charge by pointing out several things which have to be taken into account. He started by reminding the reader that Kirk's learning is extensive, but primarily in the fields of literature and history. He is a philosopher in the older sense, a "lover of wisdom," but not in the narrower, more exact sense. Zoll conceded that Kirk at times employs insufficient philosophical rigor. Zoll further believes that Kirk may have a misplaced antipathy to science and empiricism.

His social criticism and corresponding recommendations, resting as they do upon theological, historical and literary insights, would be more formidable if buttressed by the empirically-derived evidences of contemporary science. (Witalec, 2002: 261)

Zoll perhaps has a valid argument, but he probably is expecting expertise in more disciplines than it is reasonable to expect of any one person. Kirk did not present himself as a philosopher, so it is not reasonable to criticize him for not being one.

In reference to the second aspect of Kirk's thought which some can find troublesome, Zoll concedes more ground to the critics while still supporting Kirk when all has been said. His concern about Kirk was: "He assumes that the social accumulations, the 'inheritances,' are predominantly conveyed in discursive channels, especially the literary or ideational. This I tend to doubt...." (Witalec, 2002: 261)

Zoll saw this problem arising, at least in part, from Kirk's Christian metaphysics which "insists on a downward course of knowledge through the ontological hierarchy." (Witalec, 2002: 261) More than anything else, there is here a basic difference in belief. Zoll did conclude this section with a solid endorsement of Kirk for his defense of civilizational standards and the reminder that his primary value was not as a philosopher, but rather as a steward of our heritage.

Introducing the third problem area, Zoll pointed out that Kirk's religious beliefs grew stronger and deeper as his career progressed, that there is a discernable difference in the spiritual content of *A Program for Conservatives*, published in 1956, and *Enemies of the Permanent Things* which came out in 1969. Although stating that he agreed with part of Kirk's theology, he did criticize him for being content to defend a position by basing it on Christianity. Yet to Kirk and other thinkers rooted in Christianity, this is the final and highest confirmation of any position. By no means did he ignore other arguments such as those based on reason and experience, but revelation was paramount, everything else subsidiary. Zoll laments this approach, maintaining that:

> ...if one seeks to defend social recommendations by appeals to religious hypotheses, not only the social recommendations but also the religious hypotheses themselves require rational defense, unless one is again content to traffic intellectually only within the community of believers. (Witalec, 2002: 261)

Zoll manifestly is placing reason at the apex of authorities. If religious hypotheses require rational defense, then they no longer rank first. From the Christian perspective, it is perfectly valid to say that rational explanation of Christian truth is useful; it is an entirely different matter to aver that rational defense is necessary.

The last point, that Kirk is merely a nostalgic romantic, an antiquarian, was disposed of by Zoll with little effort. Kirk certainly had a love of many aspects of times past, but he functioned well and happily during the period of history in which he lived. As Zoll stated the case, a civilized person living today will regret changes such as the decline in manners and bread that is not as good, but:

> To describe this attachment to things past and lost as a quaint antiquarianism is disingenuous. One is not being either perverse or irrational in preferring Bach and Handel to John Cage or even Stravinsky. The judgment may be contentious, but it does not merely represent a clash of irrational fancies and prejudices. (Witalec, 2002: 262)

Zoll finished his analyses of allegations against Kirk with this statement of solid support; overall, he admired Kirk's defense of civilized order and freedom.

Reviewing *The Conservative Constitution* for the April 1991 issue of *Chronicles*, George W. Carey expressed general agreement with Kirk's history of the origins and early years of the United States Constitution, although he did think that Kirk overrated the influence of Burke. Carey further believed that Kirk was too sanguine about our present and future prospects for constitutional health, even suggesting that Kirk was naïve. Carey closed his review, averring that:

> In sum, contrary to what Russell Kirk asserts, there is ample evidence that the Constitution of which he writes in this book is, in fact, dead. (Carey, 1991: 35)

Carey and others certainly are free to disagree with Kirk, but naïve he was not; he saw clearly what was happening, but in the twilight of his life on earth, as his Christianity deepened, Kirk showed a growing optimism about the future.

Carey also discussed the controversy between Kirk and the Straussians (Leo Strauss and his followers) about the meaning and significance of the Declaration of Independence. This will serve as an introduction to the next part of this section.

Kirk vs. Jaffa

Between Kirk and Harry Jaffa raged an extended and sharp dispute inside the borders of conservatism, each man representing divergent branches of the movement. Jaffa, a disciple of Leo Strauss, set out to smite Kirk hip and thigh. Kirk responded on the idea level, but refused to be drawn into a personally contentious intramural feud. They had different views of the American founding, especially the Declaration of Independence, its meaning and its significance in our history. Jaffa saw the Declaration as providing a set of philosophical goals which the Constitution sought to implement. In particular, he believed that the equality clause (all men are created equal) of supreme importance. He and the Straussians in general supported government action in the raising of people to higher levels in society.

Kirk did not denigrate the Declaration of Independence, as Jaffa charged, but classified it among the key documents in American history, although he did not grant it as high a place as did Jaffa. To Kirk, the purposes of the Declaration were more modest. The document, he affirmed, set forth our grievances with the British government, making our case for independence, and, secondarily, was to appeal to France, leading to an alliance with that country against the British. It was important, but not the centerpiece the Straussians maintained it was.

Kirk rejected referring to the beginning of the United States as a "Founding" since this connotes something dramatically new, but rather, in a civilizational sense, saw a continuity of belief and principle. He supported American political independence, but emphasized the continuity between British history, culture, and traditions and the new United States which came forth from the war for independence. He understood well the problems the North American colonists had with British high-handedness and did not call for annulling the outcome of the war. But, the establishment of the United States was not an absolute break with the past as were the French and Russian

Revolutions, but rather was a political sundering rather
than a rending of civilizational fabric. The slogan "no
taxation without representation" was a British principle,
not something invented on this side of the Atlantic. Our
political and legal principles branched off the British tree.
One of the leaders in colonial Massachusetts, James Otis,
wrote *The Rights of the British Colonies Asserted and Proved*
in 1764, proclaiming that the British Constitution was the
freest that existed and that the colonists were acting to
conserve it. In *America's British Culture*, Kirk elaborated on
that principle:

> The patriots were asserting their claim to enjoy
> what Edmund Burke called "the chartered rights of
> Englishmen"—not the abstract claims of perfect lib-
> erty that would be asserted fifteen years later by French
> revolutionaries.... The American Revolution did not
> sever the links between British law and American law;
> rather, the American Republic added more chapters to
> the complex history of common law. (ABC, 34)

In addition, Kirk did not agree with Jaffa on the role
of government. To Kirk, government had a good, albeit
limited, purpose in ensuring order and justice and in pro-
tecting freedom, but it is not to be the means to inculcate
virtue. Good and truth are rooted in the church and in the
family, each of which is rooted in God. Once again, Kirk's
Christianity was a stumbling block to someone who was at
variance with his conclusions. Jaffa did not articulate any
clear understanding of the limitations imposed on human
reason and hence on human action by original sin. In
spite of agreement on some aspects of conservatism, such
as both having supported Barry Goldwater in 1964, still

between Kirk and Jaffa lay a chasm deep and unbridgeable. This controversy over our origins will carry over into the next discussion and expand into a consideration of the debate about diversity and multiculturalism.

America's British Culture

This is the title of the last book Kirk wrote which he lived to see in print. A slender volume of 122 pages, it nevertheless very effectively encapsulates his thought. In a sense, it is a summary of the much longer, 534 pages, *The Roots of American Order*. The book addresses the fad of multiculturalism and the centrifugal forces of disunity which it has unleashed. Robert Bork stated in *Slouching Towards Gomorrah: Modern Liberalism and American Decline* that:

> Had we been at the Founding a people as diverse and culturally disunited as we are today, there would have been no Founding. A Constitution and Bill of Rights would not have been proposed, and, if proposed, would have provoked a political warfare that would have torn the country too deeply for any hope of unity. (Bork, 1996: 298)

One could argue that this is an extreme statement. Perhaps it does go too far, but it definitely spoke to the need for a core of beliefs unifying a country and the grave danger of multiculturalism.

While it is true that the United States is a multiethnic country, it has not been a multicultural country. To declare that this is a multicultural country, that the basis of our culture is diversity, is meaningless. That really means that there is no national culture, that this country is just a conglomeration of separate, unassimilated groups of people. A successful country, though, must be based on voluntarily accepted values which unite people from diverse backgrounds. There must be something which transcends the differences which separate us. This Kirk recognized and addressed, writing that "A nation's traditional culture can endure only if the several elements that compose it admit an underlying unity or fidelity to a common cause." (ABC, 6)

The title, *America's British Culture*, left no doubt as to Kirk's position on multiculturalism. He cited four major ways in which our American culture has been shaped by our British heritage. The first is the English language and the great body of literature written in it. The second is the rule of law derived primarily from English law and which is outstanding in terms of individual protection. The third is representative government patterned on British institutions which began to develop during the middle ages. Fourth is a body of mores, that is, moral habits which form the ethical heritage which undergirds our culture. It was the mores of the American people which impressed Alexis de Tocqueville more than any other single factor.

Kirk was convinced that the devotees of multiculturalism are not so much motivated by a love of other cultures as they are by a detestation of Anglo-American culture in particular, Western culture in general. He ended the main text of this book on a note of optimism:

Should the multiculturalists have their way, culture, with us Americans..., would end in heartache—and in anarchy. But to this challenge of multiculturalism, presumably the established American culture, with its British roots, still can respond with vigor—a life-renewing response. Love of an inherited culture has the power to cast out the envy and hatred of that culture's adversaries. (ABC, 92)

Kirk made explicit the Christian foundation of the British North American colonies, contrasting that with the weaker faith in evidence in the United States during the late twentieth century. Especially he was appalled by the many members of the clergy who had abandoned preaching and teaching about spiritual and moral verities in favor of calling for radical changes in society, focusing on economic, political, and sociological matters (ABC, 71–73, 84).

He further was impressed by the extraordinary group of men who gathered in Philadelphia during the summer of 1787 to write the United States Constitution. They were remarkable, overall, in character, learning, and practical experience. The result was most admirable. Kirk said of what they accomplished that "The Constitutional Convention of 1787, indeed, was an achievement of representative government that never has been excelled." (ABC, 60)

A glowing tribute to Kirk and this volume was written by Ann Husted Burleigh prior to his death, but did not appear in print until after he died; it was in *Modern Age*, the summer 1994 issue. Her opening paragraph set the tone:

Any book by Russell Kirk is a feast of clarity and precision, written with authority and a touch of old-fashioned charm. As he celebrates his seventy-fifth birthday, Dr. Kirk is still paying his readers the courtesy of writing to them as intelligent laymen, worthy of strong, confident prose untarnished by either academic or journalistic jargon. He writes for the very readers who have inherited the culture he praises in *America's British Culture*, a slim book with a straightforward mission: to be a "summary account of the culture that the people of the United States have inherited from Britain." (Burleigh, 1994: 377)

Burleigh agreed completely with Kirk on the threat of multiculturalism, the firmness of our British foundation, and the need to reinvigorate it each generation.

Roger Scruton, writing in the fall 1994 issue of *The Intercollegiate Review,* also gave two thumbs up to *America's British Culture.* After summarizing the content of the book, he makes a couple of perceptive comments. The first is that actually the common law, the language, and the system of government are English. But, Scruton's point was that Kirk recognized that these had transcended their English origins. He said:

This, I believe, is what underlies Dr. Kirk's perceptive analysis of the American settlement—that it sprang from a law and a language which had already freed themselves from national boundaries, and become open to the larger world. (Scruton, 1994: 90)

Still, it must be kept in mind that Kirk never lost sight of the roots in the soil of Great Britain.

The second comment was that this book would be excellent for students as a summary of our country and its heritage. He, though, is not holding his breath waiting for that:

I doubt that it would appear on such a curriculum, however, since any student who read it would be so immediately aware of the superiority of the inheritance, that the rival "cultures" in which his teachers seek to interest him would appear quite barbaric. Indeed, that is probably what they are. (Scruton, 1994: 90)

The third review of *America's British Culture* was written by William Baer for *Reflections*, the book review supplement to *The Wanderer*, the July 1993 issue. Baer opened his review, saying that:

> At a time when Western Culture is under relentless siege, it seems perfectly appropriate that Russell Kirk, America's foremost conservative intellectual, would step forth and remind Americans of the greatness and uniqueness of our cultural foundation: our British heritage. Professor Kirk's short but brilliant new book, *America's British Culture*, is a call to arms against the radical malcontents who have dedicated themselves to undermining the morals and mores which Americans have inherited from the English people.... (Baer, 1993: 8)

He lauded Kirk's warning of the peril to a culture which loses interest in and respect for its past and his calling for us Americans to renew our appreciation for our heritage.

The Sword of Imagination

Forrest McDonald reviewed this book, the last one written by Kirk, for *National Review*, the issue of September 25, 1995. McDonald suggested that *The Sword of Imagination*, completed by Kirk shortly before his death in April 1994 and published the next year, well could be his best. He enjoyed the personal anecdotes such as Kirk's grandfather, a banker, being robbed by "Machine Gun" Kelly, one of the most famous gangsters of the 1920s and 1930s, and the account of Annette's gaining admission to the White House by presenting a tarot card with her first name written on it to a guard who mistook her for the actress Annette Funicello. He found too Kirk's accounts of people with whom he crossed paths or crossed swords absorbing and entertaining. McDonald commended Kirk for his balancing philosophical depth with lighter touches, he being sensitive to how much mental heavy going readers could take at a time.

McDonald did observe that Kirk's basic thought was set forth in earlier works such as *The Conservative Mind* and *The Roots of American Order* and would be familiar to the readers of them, but that his insights on his life and growth were fascinating. McDonald particularly was impressed by Kirk's accounts of his Greenfield Village time and his army service.

The most significant and lengthiest part of McDonald's review focused on Kirk's spiritual progression from his early days of unbelief to Christianity. This was a gradual movement, one not highlighted by a dramatic Damascus Road moment in time, but, nonetheless, a journey which ended at a sure and certain destination.

McDonald brought his review to an end with Kirk's three goals for his life, the first of which was to preserve and further the permanent things. McDonald then concluded that: "If the outlook for this end remains bleak, it is not nearly so bleak as it would have been without Russell Kirk's heroic efforts." (McDonald, 2004, p. 91)

This indeed is a tribute of note, but again it must be observed that McDonald is another conservative whose optimism for the future is rather muted. A tendency to revel in the glorious, noble, lost cause, a determination to go down bravely with all flags flying, is all too evident with some in the conservative camp. And yet, as Kirk well knew, having had to fight this tendency himself, Christianity and pessimism move in opposite directions; as the one grows the other diminishes.

Negative Responses

It took the left some time to catch on to the reality that Kirk was a foe of serious stature. After *Randolph of Roanoke* came out in 1951, the *New York Compass*, a leftist newspaper, had published a favorable review, giving Kirk an opportunity to establish himself before the left realized the threat he was. It also was true that Kirk's normally genial nature and his avoidance of personal invective generally averted, at least to some degree, intense assaults on him by those who disagreed with his views. Then too, most of his writings and speeches were on a more intellectual level than that of the general public. Even his attacks on the libertarians were phrased in a rather high-toned manner. Although, as will be commented upon later in this section, there were those personally offended by Kirk, attacks by him and most on him were not ad hominem in nature, but were based on differences in the realm of ideas, conflicts not witnessed, let alone entered into, by those whose horizons of interest do not extend much beyond having their material needs satisfied and having fun. As Donald Atwell Zoll delightfully summed up the Kirk approach to controversy:

> Even Kirk in high dudgeon—as in some essays in *Enemies of the Permanent Things*, for example, is invariably under

a refined restraint; he is a devotee of the verbal rapier in contrast to the polemical cudgel. (Witalec, 2002: 244)

Another assault on Kirk from the neoconservative direction was launched by Martin Morse Wooster in *The American Enterprise*, January/February 1996. Reviewing *The Sword of Imagination*, Wooster alleged that Kirk "never understood or appreciated capitalism" and that his conservatism was "an incomplete political philosophy, needing the fortification of an appreciation of capitalism and economics." (Witalec, 2002: 329) This too is a judgment very much in error. Anyone who has read Kirk's writings on economics knows better. Again, the problem some have with Kirk is that he placed economics within a civilizational context the parameters of which are set by Christianity.

No attempt is being made here to balance evenly positive and negative reviews of Kirk's writings. But, as a nod in the direction of evenhandedness, a few of the pokes in the eye he received will be discussed. The first was delivered by James Nuechterlein, of *First Things* who in the August/ September 1991 issue sniffed at Kirk's conservatism, arguing that it "has very little to do with American reality, but for those of a reactionary bent who imagine themselves superior to the reality, it apparently provides a congenial home." Nuechterlein proceeded on with his attempt to diminish the status of people such as Kirk as having little significant influence, alleging that "in the world of American political thought, they are little more than curiosities." (Witalec, 2002: 329)

Francis Fukuyama in his book *Trust*, published in 1995, argued that "virtually all political questions today revolve around economic ones." (Witalec, 2002: 328) He reduced religion to a useful means of providing social benefits. This may be true, but it is such a limited view that it demeans by missing the main point. This is akin to asserting that marriage is beneficial to a man because now his socks won't be left on the floor. It too may be true, but it trivializes marriage.

The Fukuyama statement on economics, his exaltation of democratic capitalism, falls far short of Kirk's support for free market capitalism as the best economic system for promoting freedom and prosperity, but that it is not an independent source of good; it is, rather, a subsidiary good when operating within a Christian framework. Apart from that, it, along with other systems of economics, cannot produce good and can give rise to corruption and exploitation.

David Frum, writing in the December 1994 issue of *The New Criterion*, extended to Kirk qualified praise, giving his opinion of the six canons of conservative thought that "Kirk expressed his major ideas in highly general terms, and so it is hard to know exactly what these six canons imply, especially the final two." He further went on that:

> Russell Kirk has always reminded me of those nineteenth-century Central European historians who promoted national consciousness by writing passionate histories of "nations" that had not existed until those same historians invented them. And just as the nationalist historians manufactured "Croatia" or "Czechoslovakia" out of half-forgotten medieval and baroque fragments, Russell Kirk inspired the postwar conservative movement by pulling together a series on only partially related ideas and events into a coherent narrative—even, although

Kirk objected to the word, into an ideology. (Witalec, 2002: 298, 300)

Frum did conclude his article, saying of Kirk that "He taught that conservatism was above all a moral cause: one devoted to the preservation of the priceless heritage of Western Civilization." (Witalec, 2002: 301)

The caveats raised by Frum concerning the six canons are difficult to comprehend unless one concludes that he simply does not like where he would be led were he to accept them.

Midge Decter, one of the most prominent neoconservatives and the wife of Norman Podhoretz, took umbrage at some comments made by Kirk in a lecture which he gave at the Heritage Foundation on December 15, 1988. Entitled "The Neoconservatives: An Endangered Species," the lecture expressed Kirk's initial enthusiasm for those now labeled neoconservatives, regarding them as liberals migrating toward conservatism. This movement started to be noticed during the period of the late 1960s into the early 1970s. Coming to be identified with it were the aforementioned Midge Decter and Norman Podhoretz, plus others including Irving Kristol, William Kristol, Ben Wattenberg, Nathan Glazer, Daniel Bell, Daniel Patrick Moynihan, and Jeane Kirkpatrick. There is a powerful Jewish component to neoconservatism, although it by no means is an exclusively Jewish movement. Kirk came to perceive, however, that the migration for many halted before crossing the bridge into conservatism. He believed the movement would cease to be within a few years, its proponents either falling back into liberalism or advancing all the way into conservatism. In this, he was wrong.

One of the remarks he made in this lecture expressed his opposition to extensive foreign entanglements by the United States. He stated that "And not seldom it has seemed as if some eminent Neoconservatives mistook Tel Aviv for the capital of the United States." (POP, 180) It should be noted that in the very next sentence he said, "Yet by and large, I think, they have helped to redeem America's foreign policy from the confusion into which it fell during and after the wars in southeastern Asia."[4] That first remark, Decter considered anti-Semitic, castigating Kirk roundly.

His record, though, does not present any valid grounds for Decter's tirade. It is true that Kirk did consider Israeli influence over our policy to be excessive. There are reasons for disagreeing with his pronouncements, but it is not likely that religious bias was his motivation. As a further point, anyone who reads that lecture will see that Kirk apparently was in a good mood that day, his rather arch humor very much in evidence from the first sentence to the last one. One can say of the remark in question that it was an unsuccessful attempt at humor and that it expresses a mistaken foreign policy position, but nothing more sinister should be charged.

An assault on Kirk rooted in liberal presuppositions was Peter Gay's in *Political Science Quarterly*, the December 4, 1953 issue. He accurately presented the contents of *The Conservative Mind*, assessing it as free from vituperation, although marred by Kirk's polemical approach, a somewhat limp compliment. Gay does concede that often radical or liberal doctrines are naïve, display philistinism, and shallowness, but he cannot accept the Kirk conservative corrective. Lionel Trilling published *The Liberal Imagination* in 1950, in which he averred that American conservatism

has no philosophy, that it is simply a grumpy response to
what they do not like. Drawing on that, Gay concluded
about *The Conservative Mind* that:

> In thus attempting to prove the existence and the moral
> and intellectual respectability of a conservative ideology,
> Mr. Kirk has only succeeded in doing the opposite; in
> trying to confute Lionel Trilling's position he has only
> confirmed it. (Witalec, 2000: 244)

John Crowe Ransom wrote an essay on Kirk and *The
Conservative Mind* which first was published in 1953
and later incorporated in his 1955 book *Poems and
Essays*. In it, Ransom is dismissive of Kirk and other
conservatives as being out of touch with the realities of
the modern age. One charge he leveled was that Kirk
failed to come to grips "with the economic responsibilities which a government has to undertake nowadays even if it is a conservative government." (Witalec,
2002: 244) There is some truth which can be dug out of
this allegation; *The Conservative Mind* does not devote
much space to economics. The thrust of that book was
in a different direction. Furthermore, although Kirk
did write a book on economics (*Economics: Work and
Prosperity*) and wove the topic into other books, still it
was not a major interest of his. But, the more substantial reason why Kirk fell short of what Ransom thought
he should have done was that Kirk believed far more in
limited government and in market economics than he
did in "the economic responsibilities which a government has to undertake nowadays." It makes no sense
to blame Kirk for not espousing policies in which he
does not believe.

Ransom concluded his essay, disdainfully asserting that:

The conservative mind is not unable, as has been charged, to learn any lessons from the changes of history. It is only unable to recite the lesson faithfully. (Witalec, 2002: 247)

On that deprecatory note, Ransom ended his essay, having consigned Kirk, he believed to the trash heap of useless thinkers.

Fiction

In 1958, T. S. Eliot wrote Kirk expressing amazement that he was authoring ghost stories, something he never would have suspected of him. This would not have been such a surprise had Eliot been familiar with the incidents from Kirk's youth recounted in the biographical section. Still, Eliot's reaction was understandable; those who had read *The Conservative Mind* well could be astonished to then read a Kirk novel or short story. To exercise an author's prerogative and here intrude myself, I too experienced something akin to that through which Eliot went. Most of the time, I keep two books going, one from which I am learning and one for pleasure such as when I am eating a sandwich or brushing my teeth. Frequently a novel occupies this second category. As much as I admired Kirk and was impressed deeply by the wisdom and brilliance found in his works, *The Conservative Mind* and *Enemies of the Permanent Things* especially, I could not imagine reading something he wrote simply to relax. Finally, after knowing him for several years and having begun my doctoral program with him, a sense of obligation propelled me into reading the first of his novels, *Old House of Fear*. To my pleasant surprise, it was a very entertaining yarn, replete with examples of people who manifested various virtues, including courage and concern for others. From that beginning, I proceeded on to his other novels and to his short stories, enthralled by the discovery of a new genre of Kirk writings and, adding to my reasons for respecting him, became astounded at his versatility.

In *Decadence and Renewal in the Higher Learning,* Kirk discussed imagery in literature and science, giving his approach to writing fiction as an example of how imagery enters in:

> When I write fiction, I do not commence with a well-concerted formal plot. Rather, there occur to my imagination certain images, little scenes, snatches of conversation, strong lines of prose. I patch together these fragments, retaining and embellishing the sound images, discarding the unsound, finding a continuity to join them. Presently I have a coherent narration, with some point to it. (DAR, 231)

Those five words, "with some point to it" almost seem to be an afterthought. Yet Kirk's novels and short stories have serious points to make, not being simply ways to entertain. Perhaps he here is being somewhat diffident. At any rate, it is fascinating to learn how well integrated was Kirk's whole being. In the creative imagination, images, scenes, recollections appear which then are formed into a narrative with a serious point, one not always made overtly, but rather one which the reader discovers. There always was at least a portrayal of good triumphing, evil failing. The clearly Christian tone became progressively more evident in the 1970s.

In his introduction to a collection of nine short stories, *The Princess of All Lands,* Kirk tied three of these stories together to form a trilogy of much the same nature as Dante's *The Divine Comedy*:

> The three concluding yarns in this book—"Balgrummo's Hell," "There's a Long, Long Trail a-Winding," and "Saviourgate,"—though written at different times and in different lands, form a trilogy with theological or transcendental implications. These are visions of the Inferno, of Purgatory, of Paradise. As Dante wrote…, in *The Divine Comedy* there lie both a literal meaning and an allegorical meaning. So it is, in their small way, with the episodes of my Dantesque trilogy. (PAL, viii)

The years when these three stories were written provide another way to trace the course of Kirk's spiritual development; the first was written in 1967, the other two in 1976.

In this same introduction, Kirk went on to say of his reasons for writing fiction:

> Why did I write these sepulchral fantasies? Why, partly to remind you and myself that we are spirits in prison: and mainly in the hope of discomforting an old man on a winter's night, or a girl in the bloom of her youth. I have dwelt in haunted houses, and I have prepared a chamber for you. If I conjure up in you a dreadful joy, like that of a small boy on a secret stair, my malice will be satisfied. (PAL, viii)

No doubt these reasons are true, tongue in cheek though they may be, Kirk having a definite sense of fun, but the probability is that his primary motivation was more that of the "theological or transcendental implications" he mentioned in the preceding quotation.

Edmund Fuller reviewed *The Princess of All Lands* for *The Wall Street Journal*, July 23, 1979. He too recounted his surprise that the author of books such as *The Conservative Mind*, *Eliot and His Age*, and *The Roots of American Order* could have been written these stories. He wrote that this "is another, and to me highly appealing, face of this learned man." Fuller moved on to comment that secular liberals do not understand adequately the origins of, the nature of, and the power of evil, that all too often sociological or psychological analyses "may rationalize away the heart of darkness, the core of the demonic.... In eerie tales, a writer, if he has sufficient perception, may take us closer to the essence of evil by symbols, images, and metaphors from the imagination."

Later in the review, discussing one of the short stories, Fuller said that here and in the other stories Kirk's "wide erudition enriches the fruits of his imagination, in both the text and the diverse epigrams at the head of each story." Fuller concluded by informing readers of this book that, in addition to learning, they will have a good time.

In contradistinction to Edmund Fuller and myself who first read Kirk's nonfiction works then discovered his world of fiction was Robert Champ who wrote in *Intercollegiate Review*, fall 1994, that he knew first the short stories then *Old House of Fear*. At that stage, he determined to learn of the other Kirk, the one who wrote *The Conservative Mind*. He found more than he imagined he would and became a voracious reader in each genre.

Don Herron wrote "Russell Kirk: Ghost Master of Mecosta" which formed a chapter in *Discovering Modern Horror Fiction*, edited by Darrell Schweitzer and published in 1986. Herron believed that during the 1960s and the

1970s Kirk developed as the preeminent author of classical ghost stories in this country. He went on to observe that Kirk, however, was known far better for his nonfiction books, articles, and lectures. Herron further commented that rarely do writers of serious nonfiction have the capacity to entertain the reader with fiction, Kirk, along with C. S. Lewis and J. R. R. Tolkien, being very much the exception. Of Kirk, Herron asserted:

> He blurs the boundaries between the real and the spiritual worlds with a skill that any fantasy writer must envy, and spins nakedly Christian yarns so well that pagan institutions like the World Fantasy Association and the Science Fiction Writers of America take him seriously at award time. (Witalec, 2000: 284)

Apparently Herron does not see the spiritual world as real. His point, though, that Kirk's stories with Christian overtones or which are overtly Christian did receive consideration from organizations not known to favor that belief system is well taken. Some of Kirk's stories were downright scary, but they never were twisted or warped so that evil triumphed and the reader was left frustrated. Nor were they amoral tales which eschewed making judgments. At this point, it will be useful to consider several of them in order to illustrate this. The trilogy of "Balgrummo's Hell," "There's a Long, Long Trail a-Winding," and "Saviourgate" will be examined first.

"Balgrummo's Hell" is set in Edinburgh, Scotland in a part of the city well past its best days. Balgrummo Lodging, the now gone to seed seventeenth-century mansion of Alexander Fillan Inchburn, tenth Baron Balgrummo, stood by an abandoned linoleum factory and a no longer used railroad marshalling yard near government housing now a slum. Fifty years ago, the baron, drawn to African witchcraft and diabolical practices in his native Scotland, had organized a horrible, bloody ritual which resulted in his being given the choice of either going on trial or accepting lifetime incarceration in his home, visited only by family, lawyers, or servants. Now, the man and the estate were much decayed, although valuable paintings still were there—A Romney, a Gainsborough, a Hogarth, a Constable, and a Reynolds, among others.

Stumbling into this apparent opportunity was an accomplished, rather sophisticated thief, Rafe Horgan. Cleverly he insinuated himself into the confidence of T. M. Gillespie, Balgrummo's attorney, learning about the house and the man frozen in time there. Gillespie told Horgan that Balgrummo is paying the price for his sins, "shut up perpetually in his box called Balgrummo Lodging, where the fire is not quenched and the worm never dieth." (PAL, 176)

Breaking into the house after knocking out the watchman, Horgan discovered Balgrummo barely alive. After taking several paintings, Horgan moved on to the chapel which had been profaned by the baron in his diabolical ritual. Behind the altar, Horgan saw an obscene Fuseli painting depicting torture, contorted forms, "the inversion of the Agony." Then, a form that looked to be Balgrummo 50 years ago came toward him:

> ...eager, eager, eager; all appetite, passion, yearning after the abyss. In one hand glittered a long knife.
>
> Horgan bleated and ran. He fell against the cobwebby altar. And in the final act of destruction, something strode across the great gulf of Time. (PAL, 180)

These words ended the story with evil punished.

"There's a Long, Long Trail a-Winding" opened with Frank Sarsfield, a 60-year-old hobo, caught by a January blizzard while trying to hitchhike in rural northern Michigan along a six-lane highway. A large, powerful, nonviolent man, he had wandered since youth, supporting himself with odd jobs, begging, and petty theft. Along the way, he had acquired snatches of learning from libraries and while in prison when caught. He had a sense of despair for his life—his theft, avoidance of trouble, even cowardice, his general rootlessness. A Roman Catholic priest, Father O'Malley, tried to reach him with assurance of God's forgiveness, that some people work out their purgatory here on earth. Sarsfield, however, believed himself unworthy of God's grace.

Desperately searching for shelter from the blizzard, through a temporary break in the snow, he saw off to the left an abandoned prison complex and to the right down a little valley, a small cluster of buildings—a church, three or four stores, and a few homes. Finding no one in the village, he moved along the main street, then espied a large fieldstone house which too was empty. The closing of the prison, the abandonment on a nearby mine, and the bypassing of the village by the highway had created a ghost town. The home had been empty for several years, but Sarsfield did find a kerosene lamp, wood for the fireplace and an upstairs stove, and jars of preserved food. He also found pictures, a memorial plaque, and an unfinished letter which told him something of the family who had lived there. Beyond these, he had a sense of having been in this place before, of having known those people at some time now long past. A dream of being with them seemed more real than reality.

Then, the second night, he returned to the dream of the previous night; again he was back in time with the family. Then Sarsfield realized he no longer was living in a dream, but somehow he had passed through the fog of time and was there in reality decades ago when past was present. A group of escaped prisoners broke into the home and threatened those he had come to love. Sarsfield no longer the coward, saved the family by killing all six attackers with an axe, but was mortally wounded himself. He opened the front door and went out to find those in his care who had fled during the fight. No one was there. Just before dying, he stumbled against a boulder with a bronze tablet that said:

> In Loving Memory of
> Frank
> A Spirit In Prison, Made For Eternity
> Who Saved Us And Died For Us
> January 14, 1915

Going back through an opening in time, Sarsfield gave his life so that others might live.[5]

The third story comprising the trilogy is "Saviourgate." Of all Kirk's short stories, this is my favorite, the one which impressed me the most with the best combination of spiritual depth, an imaginative and absorbing storyline, and interesting characters. All of Kirk's fictional works leave the reader with the sense that everything will be fine or, at least, better than it might have been, but "Saviourgate" left me with the most uplifted feeling of all.

On Christmas Eve in a northern English city, Mark Findlay, battered, discouraged, and contemplating suicide, stumbled across an inn, The Crosskeys. Inside, among the people there, was a man he recalled from 1939 in the early days of the Second World War, Ralph Bain. As their conversation progressed, Findlay was startled by Bain's inquiry about how he had died. Wondering at Findlay's incomprehension that he had crossed from the world of time into eternity, Bain had two newspapers brought out which were dated December 24, 1939 when Findlay first was there. Suspecting some sort of a hoax, he flared with anger. Bain[6], now realizing that Findlay had not died, that he was there "by some uncanny chance—or providence" for a purpose not yet understood, brought a Church of England clergyman, Canon Hoodman, into the discussion. The three of them had met at the Crosskeys back in 1939 on Christmas Eve. The Canon explained that life beyond the physical world was real, just as Findlay was experiencing it. He went on to say that:

> if you are given grace, the good things of your life are experienced, in all the fullness of your senses, whenever you desire them. True, there's another side to the coin, if you have rejected the grace of God, then the evil things of your life are forever present, and you cannot escape them. (PAL, 232)

Findlay was persuaded to spend the night at the inn. He now had decided to face his problems squarely, that "given will, given spirit, given grace," there was hope. The next morning, he left to catch a taxi to take him to the train station. Bain walked with him part of the way, then they parted. Findlay called a cab and turned back, back to vacant lots strewn with rubble and the shells of a few buildings. Bain was gone, the Crosskeys was gone. Findlay inquired of the cab driver when the street had been destroyed. He responded that a German air raid did it back in 1941. Findlay then asked the name of the street. The driver answered: "Saviourgate, sir." With that the story ended.

James Person ranked "The Invasion of the Church of the Holy Spirit" as the best of Kirk's short stories. The central character, Father Thomas Montrose, was an Anglo-Catholic priest originally from Jamaica serving an Episcopal Church parish in a run-down, crime-ridden section of an unnamed American city. The Christian tone is both direct through those who speak biblical truths and indirect through portraying the power of evil, warfare with the forces of spiritual and material darkness, and the victory of good and truth. This, though, is a darker story with characters and dialogue less well crafted than in the trilogy.

It is interesting to note that both the Episcopalian Father Montrose and the Roman Catholic Father O'Malley, traditionalists to the core, labored for orthodox Christian beliefs and practices in the teeth of determined opposition from their bishops.

Epilogue

As this section began with accolades from Kirk admirers, let it also end on the same note. Another prominent conservative scholar writing in the 1994 Russell Kirk memorial edition of *The University Bookman* was Frederick D. Wilhelmsen who set forth his conviction that:

> Before Russell Kirk published his *The Conservative Mind from Burke to Santayana* in 1953, the conservative cause in this nation was without not only a spokesman but an intelligence and imagination capable of forging into unity a new cause which was both a banner around

which men could gather despite their differences and an intellectual strategy capable of guiding its tactics for more than forty years....

In my judgment, the most influential book published in the United States on social and political philosophy within this century has been Kirk's *The Conservative Mind.* (Wilhelmsen, 1994: 18)

George H. Nash in *The Conservative Intellectual Movement in America* summed up the importance of *The Conservative Mind,* commenting that Whittaker Chambers had proclaimed it the most important book of the twentieth century. Moving on, Nash wrote that:

Here, in one fat volume, was a fervent synthesis of many conservative criticisms of the Left in the post-war years. Here was a handbook—the ideas not just of one man but of a distinguished group of men, covering nearly two centuries. Other traditions had constructed genealogies of evil men and pernicious thoughts; here, at long last, was a genealogy of good men and valuable thoughts. No longer could it be said, as John Stuart Mill had once jibed, that conservatives were the "stupid party." Thanks to Russell Kirk they could claim an intellectually formidable and respectable ancestry. Kirk had demonstrated that conservatism should be taken seriously. (Nash, 1996: 66–67)

Kirk's writings, nonfiction primarily but also fiction, by and large brought forth at least a grumbling respect for a scholarly mind and temperament. At the upper end of the scale was enthusiastic appreciation for his having woven a whole tapestry from the scattered strands of conservative thought and feeling. Since Kirk was a scholar, not a politician, an athlete, or an entertainer, it probably would be no surprise that there were people in central Michigan who were unaware of him, yet from throughout the country and around the world people came to Mecosta to learn from him and to be inspired by him.

Henry Regnery, the publisher whose company brought out *The Conservative Mind* back in 1953, wrote of Kirk in the summer 1996 issue of *Modern Age*, juxtaposing that book and Kirk's last, *The Sword of Imagination* which was published after his death. The first he praised as one of the most influential books of our time, still in print, still read, and still affecting thought. *The Sword of Imagination* he esteemed highly as the literary capstone of a memorable career:

> Few indeed have gone on to write so well their own life story, their own epitaph. In *The Sword of Imagination*, Russell Kirk capped his remarkable career with an eloquent and equally remarkable book. (Witalec, 2000: 316–317)

It is fitting to conclude discussing the reception of Russell Kirk's works by quoting praise for a book published after he had moved on from this world.

Notes

[1.] Kirk founded the journal in 1960 and edited it until his death.
[2.] Of inestimable value in considering the reception of Kirk's works was volume 119 of *Twentieth Century Literary Criticism*, published by The Gale Group, Inc., Janet Witalec project editor.

3. The letter was written September 16, 1974. The book, which came out the same year, had been sponsored by Pepperdine University.

4. Always a firm anticommunist, Kirk was not supportive of ongoing military holding actions and was dubious about our prospects for nation building in faraway lands.

5. In a later short story, "Watchers at the Strait Gate," Sarsfield returned to aid Father O'Malley in his crossing from this world into paradise.

6. In an earlier Kirk short story, "Sorworth Place," Bain had given his life to save a young widow.

5

The Relevance of Kirk

The Relevance of Kirk as Seen by Others

The late John East, university professor and United States senator, wrote of Kirk that he "was destined to become the principal intellectual founder of the American conservative movement in the post-World War II era." (East, 1986, 17) George A. Panichas, a distinguished scholar in his own right, edited a compendium of Kirk's writings entitled *The Essential Russell Kirk: Selected Essays.* In his introductory comments, he stated that "No other figure surpasses Russell Kirk in his exposition of fundamental conservative ideas in the twentieth century." (Panichas, 2007: 3)

Paul Weyrich, one of the most significant movement conservatives, completed *The Next Conservatism,* written in conjunction with William S. Lind, shortly before his death on December 18, 2008. In it, he stated of Kirk's ten principles of conservatism that "They offer as good a definition of contemporary American conservatism as we have found." (Weyrich, 2009: 11)

In the winter 1994 issue of *Policy Review,* Bruce Frohnen wrote of Kirk's legacy and relevance, stating that:

It's been 40 years and seven editions since the first publication of Russell Kirk's *The Conservative Mind.* As one observer recently put it, Mr. Kirk "is like ol' man river: he just keeps rollin' on." And so does his work. *The Conservative Mind* still is widely considered the single most influential book for modern conservatism. (Witalec, 2002: 286)

Eugene Genovese, writing in the December 11, 1995 issue of *The New Republic*, stated of *The Conservative Mind* that it "has gone through edition after edition and continues to serve the conservative movement as an exposition of principles and a history of ideas." (Witalec, 2002: 286)

How and Why

To some extent, of course, relevance is in the eye of the beholder. How significant is the legacy of someone to the individual doing the remembering and examining the record? Furthermore, when a prominent person dies, there is a period when his or her ongoing influence is proclaimed with confidence. The key consideration, though, is what that person's impact is into the second decade later. There have been innumerable famous men and women who made impressions on the times in which they lived, but left no legacy of ideas living on and guiding future generations. Even though Kirk recoiled from the idea that he or anyone would prescribe an orthodoxy of conservatism, still something of that nature is essential, a set of principles around which people can rally. This he did concisely with the six canons of conservative thought, refined later as the ten principles. From this base, conservative activists take these abiding principles and apply them to continually changing situations. Kirk simultaneously understood

this need, yet was repelled by any suggestion that he was
mandating what others must believe.

Conservative beliefs and conservative sentiments[1] are
alive and well today over 15 years after the death of Russell
Kirk in the spring of 1994. As was true during his life,
assaults on conservatism continue from many leaders in
academe, the media, politics, and popular culture. Yet a
powerful conservative current runs through our culture,
a current deriving more from Kirk than from any other
single individual of the past half century. His influence
was greater than would seem likely based on the number
of people who read his works or attended his speeches;
more significant was his impact on many who held public office, taught, and affected public opinion through the
mass media. But, it was he who in the post-World War II
West revived the conservative intellect, articulated fundamental beliefs, and showed how they applied to all aspects
of our culture.

This culture war is real and will continue as long as
human history continues. Right and truth, though, can
be strengthened, can regain much of what has been lost.
As Kirk exemplified, spiritual verities come before all else.
Then, sound thought can expand into all areas of human
activity. Absent this foundation, confusion will continue in
the conservative movement over where to draw the line,
where to stand fast. The challenges are many. For example,
arguments are presented by those who stand outside the
traditional borders of our culture that marriage between
people of the same gender should have equal merit with
that between a man and a woman, that human beings not
yet born can be killed by their mothers as a matter of individual choice; and that pornography is constitutionally
protected freedom of expression. Each of these positions

Kirk rejected on the grounds of Christian teachings, developed and applied through the creative imagination and reason.

Key to understanding Kirk's worldview was his Christianity. The mature Kirk believed firmly that Christianity was foundational for both the individual and for Western Civilization.[2] Concerning individual salvation, he set forth as his belief the orthodox position which has been proclaimed by Christians from the days of the early church. In *The Roots of American Order*, he wrote the following:

> How may a man be saved? Through faith in Christ Jesus, who descended from on high to suffer the deepest humiliation and pain for the sake of sinners. The Law reveals to man the character of sin, but only Christ can wash away sin's marks. We must be born again, through baptism, cleansed in the blood of the Lamb. No man is worthy of God's grace, yet God extends that grace. (RAO, 152)

There can be some questions raised in reference to his linking being born again and baptism, but, again, essentially this is a standard Christian affirmation, especially when one reads a few lines further his declaring that "In Christ, we find our immortality."

No utopian he, Kirk did not believe that human efforts could bring perfection into this world. Perfection is an attribute of that which lies beyond the place where we can now serve. "Truly, Christ's kingdom is not of this world. Then what hope remains? Why, the hope of the eternal City of God, where order prevails always." (RAO, 162) Institutions in this world, therefore, are imperfect. This characterization he extended to the church. Although God has promised to preserve it and even though it has a vital role to teach people of Him and lead them to Him, still it is afflicted by human corruption, being, as Kirk phrased it, but "a feeble copy of God's city." (RAO, 163)

Kirk went on to elucidate that if the church here on earth is imperfect, obviously the state is no different. It has the responsibility under God to establish order and justice so that there can be an environment within which freedom can flourish. Were the state not to exist, anarchy would be the only alternative; order, justice and freedom would vanish (RAO, 163–164). He discussed the necessity for the state and gave a common sense, balanced view of its imperfections and what the attitude of people should be when confronted by them:

> So the City of This Earth is necessary for survival in this world. Although all states are corrupt in some degree, it does not follow that every political structure is as bad as every other. It does not follow that because laws are badly executed, or perhaps badly framed, mere lawlessness would be preferable. Because many men in political life are captive to their lusts, it does not follow that divine grace is denied to all rulers or leaders of men. In the City of This Earth, we must not exact perfection. (RAO, 165)

Once again, Kirk's points are pertinent and significant. It is important to strive continually for improvement while recognizing that perfection will not be achieved in this world. In fact, demanding that human efforts produce a perfect society invariably will lead to a diminution of freedom and the imposition of dictatorship. History is replete with examples of leaders who came to power with commendable intentions, but, frustrated by the imperfections they encountered, progressively seized more and more power until they had gathered total power in their hands and justice and freedom were no more. For example, Maximillien Robespierre and the Jacobins were determined to create an ideal France by destroying the imperfect Church and monarchy and by eliminating the aristocracy, thereby purifying the country. Yet, out of this fanaticism came an autocracy worse than what the country previously had endured.

In the sixth of his canons, Kirk stipulated that change is essential for both societies and individuals since nothing can remain the same. Change for the sake of change, though, is not progress. Change can be destructive as well as beneficial. That lesson is worth learning and remembering.

Since the Fall of humankind, there never has been a time when sound thinking was in absolute control, nor has there been a time when it was nowhere to be found; the various periods have been different in terms of the relative strength of right principles. Today, conservatives often are intimidated by the electoral success of a good number of liberal candidates for public office and by the academic, media, and entertainment sectors' call for toleration of, if not full acceptance of, many ideas and practices condemned by Biblical teachings and contrary to traditional Western Civilization. Furthermore, within the conservative movement, there are those who proclaim that cultural issues, such as support for traditional marriage and for the civil rights of unborn children, should be dropped and that the conservative focus should be on limited government and economic conservatism. To Kirk, it was both and, not either or. If conservatives were to abandon their engagement in the cultural war, a war initiated by those who wish to reject the historic foundation of our civilization, then the alternative would be horrendous. Order, justice, and freedom are rooted in Christian Western Civilization, not in the absence of it. The collapse of it would be spectacular, the results of that collapse catastrophic. Of this Kirk was convinced.

Conservatism at present and in recent years has been slogging its way through an intense identity crisis. On the one side stand Russell Kirk and those of his persuasion who focus on the Christian rooted permanent things. Opposed to them is a libertarian tinged movement, looking to reason rather than to revelation and applying the laissez-faire principle to personal lifestyle choices as well as to economics. These sides can come together on some issues such as the advocacy of limited government and market economics,[3] but diverge sharply on foundational beliefs. Cooperation on these matters and common opposition to the imposition of a liberal establishment to some extent has masked the severity of the differences. But, cultural matters such as abortion, pornography, and gay issues about which there was a prevailing consensus of disapproval expressed in law, are becoming more and more controversial as advocates for them are pushing for societal approval.

Kirk was fully in accord with Eustace Percy, Lord Percy of Newcastle, who in The *Heresy of Democracy* warned of the deleterious civilizational consequences of a weakening of Christianity and a consequent growth of democracy. A firm Christian, he cautioned that "The first and fundamental character of democracy is that it is an exclusive religion." (Percy, 1955: 26) This affirmation by Percy was cited approvingly by Kirk in *Beyond the Dreams of Avarice.*

Kirk further agreed with the warnings about democratic despotism written of so effectively and eloquently by Alexis de Tocqueville in *Democracy in America.* Impressed with and optimistic about the United States, Tocqueville was concerned lest this country and others which have adopted democracy might come to exalt mediocrity, tearing down achievement and quality, that the mass would come to oppress the ambitious and capable minority. This despotism would be imposed by an all powerful central government acting in the name of the people. This government more and more would take care of the people, seducing them into no longer being interested in freedom (Tocqueville, 2000: 662–664).

Although Tocqueville, Percy, and Kirk represent separate generations, a continuity of belief runs through their thought, exemplifying the continuity of our civilization. True ideas are never dated; they always are relevant. This lesson must be renewed, perhaps learned anew, each generation. Although there are these connections linking generation to generation, there can be no resting contentedly on the achievements of those now in the pages of history. Hence, the necessity for each generation to renew and apply afresh these principles. Of this, Kirk frequently reminded people, as in canons five and six, when he wrote that civilization flourishes when faith in traditional beliefs and practices is combined with the understanding that prudent change must take place within the framework, that nothing can remain static. This should be evident to those with an appreciation of history. After all, for people to comprehend the present and prepare for the future, it is vital that they know the past. The better we understand the past the less often we will repeat the mistakes recorded there. A country whose citizens no longer are aware of their history is a country facing a grim future. An ignorant and rootless people are easier to hoodwink and control than those who have learned lessons both positive and negative, both what to do and what to avoid doing. To paraphrase George Santayana, those who refuse to learn from history are condemned to repeat it.

He believed, as did Burke, that there is a link between those living today, those now dead, and those yet unborn. Generations do not exist in isolation; each received a heritage, for good or ill, and each will pass on what it produced, for good or ill.

With keen discernment, James Person, in his biography of Kirk, observed that he had an underlying worldview and that an underlying pattern of thought ran through all his works regardless of the specific nature of each. Person wrote that:

> ...there may have been discipline-related "compartments" in Kirk's mind, but there was a sluice-gate open between each one, with certain key concepts playing a consistent part in filling them. The reader who accesses Kirk's works by way of any particular discipline, whether it be social criticism, horror fiction, economics, or whatever, will find the same philosophical underpinning supporting the thought expressed in one discipline as in another. (Person, 1999: xi)

Another area of importance where Kirk still is relevant and likely will continue to be so is education. Back in 1953, he resigned his position on the faculty of Michigan State University because the administration there had decided to lower academic standards in order to increase enrollment. The conflict between high standards and high numbers rages on. Some institutions have adhered firmly to the first, although more have opted for high numbers as the higher priority. For diverse reasons such as ethnic diversity and simply more revenue through more students, standards for both matriculation and graduation are not as rigorous as they should be at many institutions. Kirk lamented also the slippage in spiritual and moral standards as educational institutions moved away from the traditional principles of Western Civilization. Standards of behavior in schools declined as permissiveness became more widespread. More people are awakening to the danger here since for most it is manifest that a good educational system is vital for passing on the heritage of a civilization and for preparing leaders in each new generation.

Throughout his writings Kirk left no doubt that conservatism transcends national borders. Common principles link together countries whose political and judicial roots are British even though different circumstances have produced different specific applications. We in the United States have a republic with separation of powers. The United Kingdom is a monarchy with a parliamentary system. Yet we share foundational principles as to a lesser but still significant extent we do with all in Western Civilization. The relevance of Kirk's writings is not limited by time or by historical boundary.

Kirk's contributions to the revival of conservatism primarily were in the realm of thought. Although an effective speaker, he was not charismatic in voice or in appearance; his persona was not in the league of a Ronald Reagan or a John Kennedy. He did reach many people through his writings and his speeches, but it fell to others to popularize his ideas and to implement them in public policy. He generally did not prescribe specific public policy solutions; he favored limited government, but left to others precise formulas for tax rates and the size of budgets. Without thinkers in depth such as Russell Kirk, there would be no ideas to popularize or to use to change public policy.

There are those who respect Kirk, who admire his thought and his contributions to our culture, yet consider him someone whose time of greatest influence has passed. W. Wesley McDonald, who wrote an informative and often insightful biography of Kirk, does prognosticate a rather gloomy future for his influence. In this book, he wrote that "Historical conservatives such as Kirk may have lost ground within the conservative movement irrevocably." (McDonald, 2004: 211) Granted, he did qualify this assertion with the words "may have," but still an aura of pessimism rises from those words. An argument can be made that Kirk does not occupy as significant a place today among conservatives as he did during past decades, but that is not definite given the wide diffusion of his ideas directly and indirectly through those he influenced. To state that Kirk may have lost ground "irrevocably" is unwarrantedly defeatist.

McDonald then went on to discuss "Kirk's notorious aversion to modern technology." Elaborating on that by setting forth his contention that:

> His critical, and often hostile, attitude toward even some of the most beneficial achievements of modernity raise troubling questions concerning whether Kirk can be always taken seriously as a social critic and lends credence to the accusation that he frequently sought to escape from the uncertainties of the present into an idealized past. In one sense, traditionalists such as Kirk can

be correctly accused of having failed to articulate a fully developed sense of historical consciousness.... History became for him almost a sacred garden in which no room could be made for new categories of thought. His instinctive aversion to technological change, for example, led him into deploring the spread of computers, automobiles, and modern communications technologies in society rather than considering ways in which these advances could be incorporated imaginatively into a living tradition. (McDonald, 2004: 215)

This rather lengthy quotation from the writings of a professed admirer is important to consider since, were it true, Kirk's relevance would be limited. After all, if this truly were he, who would want to give much credence to the pronouncements of such an eccentric curmudgeon, someone apparently caught in a time warp? As was discussed earlier, Kirk did deplore the loss of neighborhood, especially in urban areas, to highways and the decline of reading and of creative imagination before the onslaught of television. But, he did use modern means of transportation, for example, flying around this country and to many other countries. Furthermore, he utilized modern means of communication. He had a deep love for the past; this, though, did not inhibit his functioning effectively and happily during the time in which he lived. He was a man for his time as well as the times for those yet unborn. There are no grounds for considering Kirk too out of touch to be relevant. To be fair, having written the above, McDonald did conclude his biography by stating that "Russell Kirk's books and essays, and his noble example of a life well spent, will outlast the work of his more famous contemporaries." (McDonald, 2004: 219) These words are more likely to stand the test of time and accurately describe Kirk's relevance than the earlier characterization.

The relevance of Kirk is not tied to or limited by any single issue. This is significant because a sudden change in circumstances will not render his beliefs no longer pertinent. Mark C. Henrie in *The Intercollegiate Review*, Spring/Summer 2003 insightfully commented that those thinking as did Kirk were of all American conservatives the least thrown off balance by the collapse of the Soviet Union during the period 1989–1991 (Henrie, 2003, 23n2). Kirk and his followers definitely were anticommunist and anti-Soviet oppression, but their conservatism was broader and deeper. The vicissitudes of the moment do not affect that which is truly relevant.

Keeping Lit the Flame

Annette Kirk is president of the Russell Kirk Center for Cultural Renewal in Mecosta. She works assiduously to further her late husband's heritage by promoting programs held there, traveling extensively to speak in a variety of venues, encouraging the sale of his books, co-publishing *The University Bookman* founded by him in 1960, and assisting the growing number of scholars studying him and his beliefs. People come to Mecosta from throughout this country, indeed from many other countries, making the trip to attend seminars, to study Kirk's writings, and simply to see where he lived and worked. Some of them are young people yet unborn when Kirk died in 1994. Others are adults only now for the first time encountering his thought. Still others who make this pilgrimage are well-versed in his ideas; they seek to grow in understanding them and in applying them to the challenges of the present.

The library at the Kirk Center contains over 10,000 volumes dealing with religion, history, literature, philosophy, law, politics, and economics as well as housing a continuing-to-grow archive of material by Kirk and on Kirk. It also provides facilities for seminars held there on a wide variety of topics such as "The Founders and the Constitution," "Can Virtue Be Taught?," "Recovering Historical Consciousness," and "Our Classical Patrimony." Speaking at them are such luminaries of the conservative movement as George Nash, Lee Edwards, Peter Stanlis, Jeff Nelson, Vigen Guroian, Bruce Frohnen, James Person, Wilfred McClay, Ben Lockerd, Gleaves Whitney, Ian Crowe, and Ian Boyd. At these events, Annette Kirk is the efficient organizer and gracious hostess.

Also significant in preserving and advancing the heritage of Kirk are the Heritage Foundation and the Intercollegiate Studies Institute. Established in 1973, the first named has grown to be the foremost conservative think tank in this country, very effectively bringing together "movement" conservatives from coast to coast. Russell Kirk was a natural fit with this bastion of traditional conservatism, giving close to 60 lectures for them and hosting numerous Heritage seminars in Mecosta. His name still is at the forefront there.

The Intercollegiate Studies Institute was founded in 1953 as the Intercollegiate Society of Individualists, its name and orientation representing the libertarian influence of Frank Chodorov. Over the years, it evolved in a conservative direction as the thought of people such as William F. Buckley and, especially, that of Russell Kirk moved to the fore. In 1966, the organization adopted its present name, reflecting both the change and its mission to reach, in particular, idea oriented college and graduate school students who are drawn to and influenced by a conservative message with depth, with "meat on its bones." It keeps a good number of Kirk's books in print and still holds seminars in Mecosta at the Kirk Center. He still is the most powerful single weapon in ISI's intellectual arsenal. Kirk's focus was on the principles which underlie public policy matters more than on those matters themselves. He certainly did have convictions on them, but this was not where his primary concentration was directed. He believed that if people's principles are sound and if their thought processes are working well, then their conclusions will be right. Kirk was a true believer in reference to fundamental principles, but extreme zealotry did not characterize him when it came to implementing them. He understood well that changing minds and hearts generally cannot be accomplished overnight. In a free society, people have to be persuaded, not ordered, to adopt new ways of thinking and feeling in order to effect alterations in course. This is the only means by which lasting change can be brought about. Kirk avoided the Sylla and Charybdis of, on the one hand, the fanatic who demands that everything he or she wants must be done instantaneously and, on the other, the wimpish compromiser who stands on shifting sand, who has no bedrock convictions.

An example of Kirk's rejection of extremism was his criticism of the John Birch Society, criticism going back to the early 1960s. He understood that many people attracted to it were decent conservatives motivated by love of this country, opposition to Soviet imperialism, and rejection of the domestic liberal establishment's espousal of big government. Kirk, though, believed that the organization had gone too far in seeing Communist control, influence, and conspiracies, that it was an embarrassment to the conservative movement.

Granted, there are many who disagree with Kirk or either will not or cannot delve into what he wrote or said. Developing this point further, John Attarian, in the winter 1998 issue of *Modern Age*, wrote that Kirk had not been listened to widely and that mainstream conservatives had turned more to the "American Dream," something defined mostly in economic lifestyle terms. These mainstream conservatives also were convinced that more and more the world would come to resemble the United States. Attarian further rejected the movement by these people away from the spiritual roots of our culture toward their vision of a secular utopia.

He did not abandon hope for a future revival of sound conservatism, although he teetered on the brink of doing so:

> Far from an irrelevant Tory Harrumph, Russell Kirk's political economy is now more germane, and more desperately needed, than ever. Given the scrutiny it deserves, it may redeem conservatism from a suicidal heresy. (Witalec, 2002: 329)

The conclusion is worthy, even though the anticipation of success could be more dynamic.

The Intercollegiate Review for the fall of 1994 was dedicated to "Russell Kirk: Man of Letters." One of the tributes in it was written by Vigen Guroian, entitled "*The Conservative Mind* Forty Years Later." In this essay, Guroian affirmed that this book continues to encourage us who care

> to cultivate anew the tradition of humane letters. We have diverted our attention too much from this noble endeavor. This requires renewed commitments to foster

moral and religious thought, literature and artistic creations worthy of the name. (Guroian, 1994, 25–26)

To bring to a conclusion the quotations concerning Kirk's relevance, in 1994 *The University Bookman* printed a Russell Kirk memorial edition. One of the essays was written by Frederick D. Wilhelmsen who affirmed that "Kirk's contribution to the conservative cause has not only been impressive, it has been massive, decisive. Without Kirk, the movement would never have existed." (Wilhelmsen, 1994, 18–19) That last sentence is indeed high praise, praise well earned. Kirk's disciples continue their active leadership roles in academia, in think tanks, in publishing, in the media, and in politics. The movement lives.

New challenges to right and truth continue to arise, but what is right and true does not change; it is eternal. Kirk was unswerving in standing without equivocation for "the permanent things." His books continue to be read and to focus new generations on what it takes to preserve civilization and to refurbish it. The writings of Russell Kirk will continue to be relevant as long as the commitment to order, justice, and freedom rooted in Christianity stirs the minds and hearts of people in whatever land they live.

Notes

[1.] Kirk defined sentiment as something between thought and feeling, partaking of both intellect and emotion. Patriotism is an example.

[2.] It should be remembered, as was stated earlier, that Kirk did not advocate a state church, nor did he support governmental imposition on the people of what they must believe theologically.

3. For example, Kirk did appreciate aspects of Ludwig von Mises' philosophy such as his opposition to big government and for the contributions to freedom and prosperity springing forth from market economics. But, he deeply disagreed with the orientation of von Mises to reason rather than to the deeper Christian roots of our civilization (PFC, 145–147).

Bibliography

Bork, Robert H. (1996) *Slouching Towards Gomorrah: Modern Liberalism and American Decline.* New York: Regan Books.

Brownson, Orestas A. (2003) *The American Republic: Its Constitution, Tendencies, and Destiny.* Wilmington, Delaware: ISI Books.

Buckley, William F. (ed.) (1970) *Did You Ever See a Dream Walking?: American Conservative thought in the Twentieth Century.* Indianapolis, Indiana: The Bobbs Merrill Company, Inc.

East, John P. (1986) *The American Conservative Movement: The Philosophical Founders.* Chicago: Regnery Books.

Edwards, Lee (1999) *The Conservative Revolution: The Movement that Remade America.* New York: The Free Press.

Gottfried, Paul and Fleming, Thomas (1988) *The Conservative Movement.* Boston: Twayne Publishers.

Hamilton, Alexander, Madison, James and Jay, John (2003) *The Federalist Papers.* New York: Signet Classic.

Hart, Jeffrey (2005) *The Making of the American Conservative Mind: National Review and Its Times.* Wilmington, Delaware: Intercollegiate Studies Institute.

Kirk, Russell (2002, first edition 1957) *The American Cause.* Wilmington, Delaware: Intercollegiate Studies Institute.

— (1993) *America's British Culture.* New Brunswick, New Jersey: Transaction Publishers.

— (2004) *Ancestral Shadows: An Anthology of Ghostly Tales.* Grand Rapids, Michigan: William B. Eerdmans Publishing Company.

— (1990) *The Conservative Constitution.* Washington, D. C.: Regnery Gateway.

Kirk, Russell (2001, first edition 1953) *The Conservative Mind.* Washington, D. C.: Regnery Publishing, Inc.

— (1966) *A Creature of the Twilight: His Memorials.* New York: Fleet Publishing Corporation.

— (1978) *Decadence and Renewal in the Higher Learning.* South Bend, Indiana: Gateway Editions.

— (1999) *Economics: Work and Prosperity.* Pensacola, Florida: A Beka Book.

— (1997, first edition 1967) *Edmund Burke: A Genius Reconsidered.* Wilmington, Delaware: Intercollegiate Studies Institute.

— (1971) *Eliot and His Age.* New York: Random House.

— (1984, first edition 1969) *Enemies of the Permanent Things: Observations of Abnormality in Literature and Politics.* La Salle, Illinois: Sherwood Sugden and Company.

— (1993) *The Politics of Prudence.* Bryn Mawr, Pennsylvania: Intercollegiate Studies Institute.

— (1979) *The Princess of All Lands.* Sauk City, Wisconsin: Arkam House Publishers.

— (1989, first edition 1962) *A Program for Conservatives.* Washington, D. C.: Regnery Gateway.

— (1996) *Redeeming the Time.* Wilmington, Delaware: Intercollegiate Studies Institute.

— (1977, first edition 1974) *The Roots of American Order.* La Salle, Illinois: Sherwood Sugden and Company.

— (1995) *The Sword of Imagination: Memoirs of a Half-Century of Literary Conflict.* Grand Rapids, Michigan: William B. Eerdmans Company.

— (1987) *The Wise Men Know What Wicked Things Are Written on the Sky.* Washington, D.C.: Regnery Gateway, Inc.

Maine, Sir Henry Sumner (1976) *Popular Government.* Indianapolis, Indiana: Liberty Classics.

McDonald, W. Wesley (2004) *Russell Kirk and the Age of Ideology.* Columbia, Missouri: University of Missouri Press.

Nash, George H. (1996) *The Conservative Intellectual Movement in America: Since 1945.* Wilmington, Delaware: Intercollegiate Studies Institute.

Pafford, John M. (2003) *On the Solid Rock: Christianity and Public Policy*. La Grange, California: Center for Cultural Leadership.

Panichas, George A. (ed.) (2007) *The Essential Russell Kirk: Selected Essays*. Wilmington, Delaware: Intercollegiate Studies Institute.

Percy, Eustace (Lord Percy of Newcastle) (1955) *The Heresy of Democracy: A Study in the History of Government*. Chicago: Henry Regnery Company.

Person, James E. (1999) *Russell Kirk: A Critical Biography of a Conservative Mind*. Lanham, Maryland: Madison Books.

Rousseau, Jean Jacques (1952) *The Social Contract*, vol. 38 of *Great Books of the Western World*, Hutchins, Robert Maynard (ed.) Chicago: Encyclopedia Britannica, Inc.

Rusher, William A. (1984) *The Rise of the Right*. New York: William Morrow and Company.

Russello, Gerald J. (2007) *The Postmodern Imagination of Russell Kirk*. Columbia, Missouri: University of Missouri Press.

Steinfels, Peter (1979) *The Neoconservatives: The Men Who Are Changing America's Politics*. New York: Simon and Schuster.

Story, Joseph (1851) *Commentaries on the Constitution of the United States*. Boston: Charles C. Little and James Brown.

Tocqueville, Alexis de (2000) *Democracy in America*, trans. and ed. Mansfield, Harry C. and Winthrop, Debra. Chicago: University of Chicago Press.

Viereck, Peter (1956) *Conservatism from John Adams to Churchill*. Princeton, New Jersey: D. Van Nostrand Company, Inc.

Viguerie, Richard A. (1981) *The New Right: We're Ready to Lead*. Falls Church, Virginia: The Viguerie Company.

Weyrich, Paul M. and Lind, William S. (2009) *The Next Conservatism*. South Bend, Indiana: St. Augustine's Press.

Witalec, Janet (ed.) (2002) *Twentieth Century Literary Criticism*. Farmington Hills, Michigan: Gale Research.

Index